TOWN MEMOIRS

Newburyport

Stories from the Waterside

town memoirs (toun mem'wärs). 1. True stories that capture the spirit of a community, its genius loci. 2. Anecdotes passed on within a community from generation to generation. 3. A series of books by regional storytellers, illustrated by local artists, preserving the popular history of great American towns

The Dreadnaught *washed up on the rocks of Cape Penas, northeast of Tierra del Fuego in South America. When the captain saw no hope of saving her, he and the crew lowered the boats.*

Newburyport

Stories from the Waterside

By Liz Nelson

Illustrated by Christopher Gurshin

Commonwealth Editions
Beverly, Massachusetts

♣

To my husband, Philip

Designed by Janis Owens

Published and distributed by Commonwealth Editions,
an imprint of Memoirs Unlimited, Inc.,
21 Lothrop Street, Beverly, Massachusetts 01915.

Visit our website: www.commonwealtheditions.com.

Printed in the United States of America

Contents

❧

Twentieth Century

Acknowledgments

❦

I am enormously indebted to many people, most of whom live in Newbury, Newburyport, or West Newbury. Without them I could never have written this book. I thank them for so graciously giving their time and sharing their stories and knowledge of the community. Sadly, not all stories could appear between the covers of this book, but each deepened my understanding of Newburyport. My heartfelt thanks to Thomas Ambrosi, Nancy Ames, Mae Atkinson, Ruth Burke, Marjorie Cary, George Cashman, Dr. Marc Cendron, Dick Cunningham, Chip Davis, Ralph Devone, Chief Stan Dixon, Norman Doyle, Dr. Ambler Garnett, Jr., Elizabeth Gillette, Robert Henneberry, Roxie Kalashian, Dorothy LaFrance, Prof. Benjamin Labaree, Susan Little, Marjorie Lynn, Byron Matthews, Pete Morse, William O'Flaherty, Lorraine Ott, John Pramberg, Jr., William Quill, Mark Sammons, Christopher Snow, Rev. Bertrand Steeves, John and Kay Walsh, Josiah Welch, Jay Williamson, Connie Wood, and, last and most, Gregory Laing and Todd Woodworth, Newburyport's storytellers par excellence.

I extend another large thank-you to Gregory Laing

and Todd Woodworth, for reading and commenting on the manuscript. I apologize for any errors that remain; they are my responsibility.

The staff of the Newburyport Public Library welcomed me and was always ready to assist me. I especially thank Cecile Pimental of the Hamilton Room and the volunteers who work there for so patiently helping me dig for details. My thanks also to the staff of the Boxford Public Library for tracking down so many books for me.

Friends and writers Barbara Wilson and Karen Marzloff I thank for keeping me writing, offering thoughtful critique, and acting as my word police.

I thank my husband and three sons for sharing in the excitement and for their ever-present support and humor, even when one of them had to make dinner. Special thanks to my son Peter who helped with the research.

My warm thanks to my grandmother, the family storyteller, at whose side I heard so many tales.

Watching Chris Gurshin capture moments from the stories in his illustrations was a delight, as was working with him. And last, but definitely not least, I thank Webster Bull, editor and publisher, for his trust, enthusiasm, support, and skill.

—Liz Nelson
March 2000

Eighteenth Century

How did Timothy Dexter, the tanner, make a fortune large enough to afford mansions and "museums"?

Lord Timothy Dexter

ᘓᕲ

Twenty-year-old Timothy Dexter arrived in Newburyport in 1767 with ten dollars in his pocket. Over two hundred years later, his legend remains among the town's richest.

Having completed his apprenticeship as a tanner, this son of a Malden farmer came to partake in Newburyport's surging prosperity. Within three years, he had married a widow of comfortable means, moved into her home near Market Square, and set up a leather goods shop, "Sign of the Glove."

Twenty years later, he was successful enough to buy one of the most elegant houses in town, the Tracy mansion on State Street. He moved to Chester, New Hampshire, for a short period in 1796, and to his delight the neighbors there nicknamed him Lord Timothy. He brought the title back with him to Newburyport and before the century ended became grander still. He took up residence at 201 High Street in a house previously owned by Jonathan Jackson, who had been one of the town's wealthiest shipowners.

Though no one can claim that Lord Timothy had been idle in creating a reputation before he reached High Street, it was there that he added the finishing touches. He painted his stately Federalist mansion white, which was quite acceptable, but trimmed it in green, which was not. He ordered turrets for the roof and placed enormous gilded balls on the corners. On the peak, he built a splendid cupola on which perched an eagle, wings spread. This was all a bit much, but Old Money has always known that New Money cannot necessarily buy good taste.

In his well-tended gardens, he built a tomb. Over it stood a twelve-foot-square, eleven-foot-high glass structure he called the Temple of Reason. He had a casket built by a local cabinetmaker (mahogany, of course, with brass trimmings and a lock on the inside). Painted white inside and out, it also was trimmed in green. People say Dexter liked to rest in his coffin, and he was known to take naps in his tomb.

With everything in place, he planned a mock funeral to see how the living would react to his death. He sent out invitations, opened his grounds to the public, and dressed his family in mourning attire. As the funeral procession led by the casket made its way to the tomb, Dexter watched from upstairs. Story has it, he was displeased by his wife's apparent lack of grief.

Lord Timothy was just warming up. At the start of the new century, he began to transform his property into a museum so that people (as he wrote in his inimitable style) could "see what has bin in the world grate wase back, to our own forefathers . . . to sho 45 figers, two leged and fore leged, becos we cant doue well without fore Leged. . . . "

Forty statues of men he admired adorned his property. Each hand-carved, colorfully painted figure stood eight feet tall, the work of a local craftsman whose usual fare was figureheads for the prows of ships. George Washington presided from an arch over the central doorway. John Adams flanked him on one side, Thomas Jefferson on the other. The rest—Napoleon Bonaparte, King George, John Hancock, and Louis XVI among them—stood on tall columns in Dexter's front garden, along with a number of giant lions.

How did Timothy Dexter, the tanner, make a fortune large enough to afford mansions and "museums"? Hard working and with a shrewd eye for business, he began trading on a small scale early on and saved his profits. With uncanny foresight, after the Revolutionary War ended, he invested his money in Continental dollars, which could be bought at a steep discount. When Alexander Hamilton established a national monetary system, "Continentals" became worth their full face value. Overnight, Timothy Dexter became a rich man. Soon after he moved into the Tracy mansion, he became the owner of two ships and continued to expand his wealth through trade. He wrote, "I was very lukky in spekkelation."

While activity on his museum proceeded outside his mansion walls, inside he worked to further his reputation. In case anyone had not been informed of the details of his life, he wrote an autobiography (sort of), titled *A Pickle for the Knowing Ones*. In it he expresses his views on mankind, religion, his wife, and world politics (he thought an international legislative body would be good) and, of course, tells of his life.

Lord Timothy was known as a savvy man of business, but some of his transactions were peculiar indeed. In his booklet he describes his most famous one. For three consecutive nights, he insists, he dreamed that warming pans would sell well in the West Indies. Since the pans were used in New England to warm beds on frigid winter nights, it seemed unlikely that anyone in the Caribbean would need one. Lord Timothy claims, however, that he imported 42,000 of them from England, shipped them south, and made a huge profit. How? With the cover removed, a warming pan was a perfect utensil for straining molasses, an important Caribbean product.

Not only did the content of his booklet cause readers to shake their heads, so did the format. As the quotes above show, Lord Timothy's spelling was atrocious, and he had no use for punctuation. After the first printing sold out, he amended the second edition. He inserted a page of punctuation marks at the end with the note: "Nowing ones complane of my book the fust edition had no stops I put in a Nuf here and thay may peper and solt it as they plese"

. . ; , " , , . ; . . . . , , , " . . . , . ; . , ? . , , ?" ". , . ,
; ; , , . . ? ", , . ."

Just as his writing lacks periods and commas and his spelling is inventive, Lord Timothy's life story contains blanks that can never be filled and includes tales that may be the product of the imagination (his own or the teller's). No one can prove

*The economic well-being of the port has always had a direct impact on
rural Newbury.*

or disprove the story of the warming pans—or any other of Lord Timothy's trades—because the Great Fire of 1811 reduced the Custom House and its records to ashes. On the other hand, there seems to be little doubt that he was a lecherous alcoholic. He returned to Newburyport from Chester in part because a lawyer severely beat him for inappropriate behavior with the lawyer's lady friend. His lordship gave his wife $2,000 to leave him, people say, then another $2,000 to come back. In his favor, he paid debts promptly and was always fair to those who worked for him. (Although there is that story about the painter who refused to follow erroneous orders regarding Thomas Jefferson's statue. Story has it that Lord Timothy became so enraged he shot at him, but he probably paid him, too.)

Like many philanthropists then and now, Dexter offered to pay for improvements to the town (by building a new brick market house and paving High Street) if they were renamed Dexter Hall and Dexter Street, respectively. The town thanked him but declined. High Street remained unpaved for another fifty years, and the side street next to his mansion *is* now named Dexter Lane. Lord Timothy gave money to churches for interior improvements and bells. And finally, in his will, he left $2,000 to the town from which the interest was to be distributed annually to the poorest citizens of Newburyport. Timothy Dexter had not forgotten what it was like to walk into town with only ten dollars to his name.

Lord Timothy Dexter died on October 26, 1806, with, we're told, the key to his coffin in his pocket. He left us his book, which has been reprinted twelve times, and stories that get better with each retelling.

Breakaway from Newbury

ভ৩

Four years before Timothy Dexter came to town, signatories of the petition of 1763 claimed that they were not represented fairly and that they paid a disproportionate amount in taxes. Furthermore, they insisted that they got little for their taxes: no public schools, no fire engines, no road repairs. Who were these men? Colonists complaining to the British? No.

They were the "waterside" people living in close vicinity to the Merrimack River, and they were fed up with the rest of the town of Newbury. Outnumbered by the farmers of the rural community, the merchants, traders, and mariners who lived along the river wrote to the colonial government asking for a "division of the town into separate communities." The legislature and governor agreed, and in February 1764, Newburyport, the smallest town in Massachusetts, comprised of only 647 acres, was incorporated.

Since land equaled wealth in an agricultural economy, many scoffed at this tiny new community of 2,882 inhabitants. They could not foresee the leading role the town would play in international trade in just two decades and the wealth this would bring. At its inception, Newburyport had three shipyards along the Merrimack River. By the mid-nineteenth century, three blocks of Newburyport waterfront would have one of the greatest concentrations of shipyards along the entire Atlantic coast. Newburyport ships not only sailed around the world, they also were sold all over the world. And no one could have predicted that the town would give birth to eminent lawyers, professors of law, and justices of state and federal courts. Tristram Dalton, the first U.S. senator from Massachusetts following the adoption of the Constitution came from Newburyport, as did entrepreneurs, inventors, reformers, and artists. For almost two and a half centuries, Newburyport has been home to independent-minded people who assessed trouble from all sides and found solutions to daunting challenges.

Newbury and Newburyport became separate political entities in 1764, but the two communities carried a shared history into the future. Families intermarried. The economic well-being of the port has always had a direct impact on rural Newbury. The boundaries changed once again in 1851, and Newburyport gained more than 2,800 of Newbury's citizens. While the stories in this book focus on Newburyport, just as the name Newbury is embedded in Newburyport, so are the people of Newbury very much present in the pages that follow.

Why ship what floats?

Some creative and frugal Newburyporters, observing that wood floats, were determined to transport lumber to England without a ship. Their method was to tie the timber together to create a sturdy raft, roughly shaped like a ship. In the middle, they made space for a few (utterly crazy) men and their provisions. With primitive sails rigged, away went the "vessel." A London newspaper reported in 1770 that one of these rafts crossed the ocean in just twenty-six days.

Missing remains

British evangelical preacher Rev. George Whitefield spoke passionately and eloquently, drawing such large crowds that many of his sermons had to be held outdoors. He would sometimes preach three or four times a day, and it is estimated that he gave close to 18,000 sermons during his life. His Calvinistic views, however, were quite controversial. On his first visit to what was then still Newbury, in 1740, only one church, the one in Market Square, would allow him to preach.

Whitefield traveled constantly, coming to the colonies seven times, and was a frequent visitor to Newbury and Newburyport. In fact, he died at the Reverend Jonathan Parson's home on School Street exactly thirty years after he first came here. Portsmouth and Boston followers wanted the honor of burying him in their towns. Friends in England wanted his body shipped home. Instead, his remains were laid to rest in a vault under the pulpit in the First Presbyterian Church on Federal Street in Newburyport. In keeping with his desires, he was buried in his gown, cassock, bands, and wig.

The coffin lid stood open so that visitors could view his remains. Many came, and one did not leave empty-handed. In 1829, the church was remodeled and Whitefield's bones, and those of Reverend Parsons (first pastor of the church) and Reverend Prince (a close friend of both), were placed together in a new brick crypt. Reverend Whitefield's right arm was missing.

Story has it that a great admirer simply had to have some relic of the beloved preacher. He paid a friend who, with the help of the sexton's son, took the bones. When word spread on both sides of the Atlantic, people were outraged by such desecration.

It took twenty years, but apparently the bone-thief needed to make amends. He entrusted a box to the care of a Newburyport captain, insisting that he promise to see the arm restored to the crypt with his own eyes. The captain delivered the package, which included an explanatory and apologetic letter, to the minister of the church. The remains now lie intact, with those of the other two ministers, in a closed coffin below the church pulpit.

"All men born free and equal"

✌

In 1755 a Newbury town census counted fifty slaves. Mixed in with the barley, cows, and flax, slaves were routinely listed as part of an estate's inventory. For example, upon his death in 1711, Newbury resident Henry Rolfe left, among other "items":

Fifteen sheep, old and young	£3 15s
An old gun	£0 2s
An old negro man	£10

William Davenport, owner of the Wolfe Tavern in Newburyport, died in 1773 and passed on to his heirs:

one negro woman	£3
one ditto child	£7
160 gals. West India Rum	£21 6s 8p
18 gals. Wine	£4 16s
20 gals. Cherry Rum	£2

The Wolfe Tavern, on State Street, had for several years been the favored place in town for political gatherings, and the Newburyport men who marched to fight at Bunker Hill first assembled there. As the colonists became more fervent concerning their own rights to liberty, many of them applied the same logic to the issue of slavery.

In fact, slaves brought suit against their owners throughout Massachusetts and won their freedom in court. In Newburyport, Caesar, a black slave, took this process one step further. In October 1773, John Lowell filed suit on Caesar's behalf against Richard Greenleaf, seeking not only Caesar's liberty but also punitive damages of £50. The jury ruled in the black man's favor and awarded him £18 plus costs. His case was the first and possibly the only one of its kind in Essex County. A few years later John Lowell moved from Newburyport to Boston, where he was chosen as one of the twelve delegates to frame the Constitution of the Commonwealth of Massachusetts. He is the author of the clause in the state Bill of Rights that abolishes slavery.

Newburyport Tea Party

Legend has it that Eleazer Johnson, a prominent shipbuilder in Newburyport, led a band of patriots who seized tea and burned it in Market Square three days *before* the men of the Boston Tea Party performed their famous deed. It is written that Johnson called to the men working for him to "knock your adzes from the handles, shoulder the handles and follow me." He then shouldered his tool and proceeded at the head of the group to the

Eleazer Johnson, a prominent shipbuilder in Newburyport, led a band of patriots who seized tea and burned it in Market Square three days before the men of the Boston Tea Party performed their famous deed.

powder house. The door of the building yielded very nicely to his swing of the adz, and each man took a chest of tea and marched to Market Square. There the adz was once again of service, and soon tea spilled out of the chests. The men piled it all into one big heap, and up it went in flames. Johnson's descendants passed down his adz from one generation to the next. It can now be seen at the Cushing House Museum.

The British are coming?

Immediately following the confrontation between the Minutemen and British troops at Lexington on April 19, 1775, citizens feared retaliation. Two days later, word spread from Ipswich as rapidly as horses could gallop: the British had sailed up the Ipswich River and were rampaging through the town, killing all in sight. People in neighboring communities abandoned their homes, clogging the roads headed north. One panicked woman fled carrying her baby protected snugly against chill spring winds. About four miles up the road, she stopped to nurse the infant on the steps of the meetinghouse in what is now Newburyport, but when she removed the wrappings, out leaped her cat. She had left the baby home. The rumor regarding British troops proved to be completely false, and the incident became known as The Ipswich Fright.

Privateers

Sails furled, the British brig *Sukey* lay tied along the wharf. A stranger may have wondered why no colors fluttered from her mast. Locals, however, knew that on this day, January 15, 1776, Newburyport privateers, having captured the enemy vessel and lowered her flag, had brought her in and gleefully emptied the cargo of food meant for British troops in Boston.

The day was still young, and men looking out over the bay noted another ship flying British colors tacking back and forth without any apparent purpose. Wind-whipped whitecaps warned of inclement weather. The men watching concluded the ship was lost, perhaps confusing Ipswich Bay for Boston Harbor, which was under British control.

Having hatched their plan, seventeen Newburyporters set out in three small whaleboats to offer their "assistance." As they neared the ship, their leader, Offin Boardman, called out asking whence they sailed and whereto bound.

"London to Boston," came the answer. "And where might you be from?"

"Boston," Boardman lied and offered to pilot the ship *Friends* to port.

Within minutes, he boarded, unarmed. While he exchanged pleasantries with the British captain, his companions secured their boats and clambered aboard, too. They, however, were well armed. To the captain's astonishment, as soon as the colonists were on deck, Boardman called for the colors to be struck. Thus, without firing a single shot, Newburyport privateers brought in their second ship that day. From the time they set out to the time they docked, only six hours had elapsed.

Privateers were simply state-sanctioned pirates. To prevent supplies from reaching English troops, the Continental Congress authorized private shipowners and their crews to capture enemy vessels. This they were delighted to do, not only for patriotic reasons, but because the cargo became theirs to divide and sell. *Friends* turned out to be carrying over three thousand bushels of coal; pork, alive in the form of hogs and dead in the form of eighty-six pork shoulders; and many casks of porter, vinegar, and sauerkraut.

The captains of the two captured ships stayed at the Wolfe Tavern for a while. Captain Bowie of *Friends* returned to

England. Captain Engs of the *Sukey* not only remained in Massachusetts, he later went on to command a privateer sailing out of Newburyport.

Blockaded

ᘒᘓ

Privateering profits exceeded investors' wildest dreams during the early years of the Revolutionary War. Nathaniel Tracy, principal owner of 134 merchant vessels and armed cruising ships, captured 120 British ships, took 2,225 prisoners of war, and sold ships and cargo for almost $4 million.

At first, the Royal Navy did not seem to take these seagoing rebels seriously. In time, however, they saw their error and created blockades that were virtually impenetrable. By the war's end, British naval forces had inflicted heavy damages on the colonists' shipping fleet. Nathaniel Tracy, for example, once one of Newburyport's wealthiest men, was left with just 14 of his 134 vessels and with debts almost as great as his profits had been just a few years before.

Madam Hooper, witch

ᘒᘓ

From the start, anyone could tell that Madam Hooper was different. She arrived in Newbury around 1760 with a wardrobe so extensive and elaborate that story has it she never bought another piece of clothing. This, of course, made her short, stout figure easily recognizable on any street in town. And if anyone needed further proof of her peculiarity, it rested in her mouth: she had a full set of double teeth.

In spite of her teeth, people also noted her advanced level of education and apparent good breeding, and they invited her to teach. Yet it was not for molding the minds of the young that Madam Hooper gained her reputation, but rather for her impact on those who should have been less gullible. She adopted a mysterious manner of speaking mixed with prophetic utterances, and over time she earned a reputation as a most reliable fortuneteller. She drew clients from near and far, including Lord Timothy Dexter, and as she listened to them, she held their attention with her alert green-gray eyes. To the questions of some, she would respond with impenetrable silence. Others heard predictions that proved to be uncannily accurate.

Some began to refer to Madam Hooper as "the witch." For intelligent company, or perhaps to add to the aura, she kept a black chicken as her pet. Her "familiar" with clipped beak and claws followed her about town. Children ran when she approached. Adults treated her with scrupulous courtesy, since it would never do to offend someone with supernatural powers. As a result, Madam Hooper, the fortuneteller, lived her life free of eighteenth-century restrictions, coming and going whenever and wherever she pleased.

According to local lore, one day someone placed two knitting needles in the form of a cross in front of Madam Hooper. It is said that she stayed in her seat for hours, thus confirming that she was possessed, for *everyone* knows that no witch can pass over a cross. Then again, perhaps Madam Hooper didn't want to give anyone an excuse to doubt her powers. We're told she died in poverty and degradation. The storytellers offer no further details, so we don't know whether the ending is meant to serve as a warning against being different, or whether it is the truth.

Revenue cutter *Massachusetts*

⌘

In 1790, Secretary of the Treasury Alexander Hamilton proposed that the fledgling United States create a Revenue Cutter Service to ensure that ships pay all import tariffs. Congress passed the bill establishing the service on August 4 and commissioned the building of ten vessels. In 1791, Newburyport built the first and largest of the fleet of revenue cutters, the fifty-foot-long *Massachusetts*. Each revenue cutter patrolled the coast for smugglers and inspected incoming ships for both cargo and the health of the crew. The cutter would then escort the merchant ship to the Custom House. The original Revenue Cutter Service is one of five federal services, including the Lighthouse Service and the Life Saving Service, that presently make up the U.S. Coast Guard. On August 4, 1958, the Honorable A. Gilmore Flues, Assistant Secretary of the U.S. Treasury, and several other dignitaries arrived to unveil the monument commemorating Newburyport as the official birthplace of the Coast Guard.

How much to cross the Merrimack?

Newburyport shareholders, Timothy Dexter among them, built the first bridge to span the Merrimack River in 1792. It stood where the Chain Bridge now stands, just east of today's Route 95. The toll bridge had competition from the ferries, however, which had operated for decades. The first ferry began service in 1641 via Carr's Island to Salisbury. A man, calf, yearling, or hog could cross for two pence. Cattle and horses cost six pence each, but a goat cost only a penny. If the ferry was too full and a horse had to swim across, his owner paid nothing for his own boat ride.

The two R's

Children who believe life would be so much nicer if math ceased to exist should have lived in Newburyport in 1792. In May of that year, the town voted to eliminate arithmetic in the two outlying elementary schools. Only the center school continued to teach its young citizens how to add, subtract, multiply, and divide.

Ben Franklin pays a visit
❧

In 1801, the members of the First Religious Society determined that their seventy-five-year-old meetinghouse in Market Square was beyond repair, so they dismantled it and built a new church on Pleasant Street. However, the rooster weathervane that is still seen atop the graceful 159-foot spire comes from the old steeple, along with its story.

Lightning struck the steeple of the old meetinghouse in 1754. And where lightning struck, Benjamin Franklin often followed. He came to what was then still Newbury and carefully examined the weathervane, the bell and its iron hammer that struck each hour, and, most particularly, the fine wire that hung twenty feet down from the bell. Above the bell, lightning had shattered the church spire, but no further damage was evident over the length of the wire. In a paper read before the Royal Society in London, Franklin concluded that even the smallest wire will conduct electricity, and that if the wire had extended from the tip of the steeple down into the ground, the church tower would not have been damaged at all.

The weathervane did undergo one minor alteration. A piece of iron has been welded to the back, and three prongs extend above. While Benjamin Franklin may not have done this work himself, but rather left instructions, historians agree this is probably one of his first attempts at making a lightning rod.

Nineteenth Century

Something slammed against the house, every inch of which shuddered. The family gripped each other in terror, and then it was gone as suddenly as it had come upon them.

Tornado!

❧

The Newbury and Newburyport area has recorded hundreds of earthquakes, but tornadoes are quite rare. One blew through on September 22, 1802. On a still, humid night Sallie Little and her family retired to bed, listening to a steady rainfall drumming their farm roofs. At midnight she awoke to torrents of water beating against the house, while lightening and thunder competed for attention. The family huddled in the kitchen in total darkness.

Then a roar approached, which years later Sallie would compare to the magnified sound of a train. Something slammed against the house, every inch of which shuddered. The family gripped each other in terror, and then it was gone as suddenly as it had come upon them.

Within an hour, moonlight beamed from between breaking clouds onto a scene no farmer and his family ever want to see. Half the house roof and one-third of the long barn roof were gone. The cider mill had been torn off its foundation and put down a hundred feet away. Fences lay strewn on the ground, but perhaps worst of all, the wind had ripped up over seventy trees in the orchard. Sallie's father returned inside and buried his face in his hands.

Several neighboring farms also sustained damage, and the tornado touched down on a wharf along the river, too, leveling a small building. Word spread fast and townspeople from both Newbury and Newburyport came, tools in hand, to help those in need. The tornado had cut its path on Wednesday night. By sunset on Saturday, every damaged building had a roof, and each tree had been reset in place. The uprooted trees grew at odd angles but continued to bear fruit as well as ever. Only fences still called for repair, and odds and ends needed to be picked up. One such "end" was a wheel by the Littles' back door. It belonged to a fully laden hay cart that had stood in front of the barn Wednesday evening. It was the only remnant of that cart ever found.

On chamber pots, too

Quite possibly, James Akin had days when he wished he had never set foot in Newburyport, and Edmund Blunt must have felt the same way. Akin, an accomplished engraver born in South Carolina, arrived in town in 1804. A year later, Blunt, a publisher, hired him to engrave some maps and charts. They quarreled over some details in the work, and Akin slapped Blunt in public at a hardware store. Enraged, the publisher grabbed a cast-iron skillet and threw it at Akin, who ducked. The skillet smashed through the window and hit Captain Nicholas Brown, who was merely passing by.

Akin promptly set to work on a copperplate engraving titled *Infuriated Despondency*. The caricature showed Blunt in the act of heaving the skillet at the artist. Captain Brown helped Akin make the arrangements to send the engraving to Liverpool, England, to have manufacturers of crockery reproduce the caricature on pitchers, washbowls, and chamber pots. Large quantities of this crockery were shipped back to Newburyport where, as soon as word got out, Blunt's friends purchased and smashed most of it.

Akin also reproduced the engraving on bookcovers for children and advertised them in the *Newburyport Herald* as works intended "to amuse their juvenile fancy." Blunt struck back by filing a libel suit against Akin. The bitter fight continued until the case was decided in Akin's favor. Two years later, he returned to Philadelphia, where he had worked earlier, and continued his career as a successful engraver.

Slow down!

ℰↃ

N EWBURYPORT—MAY 13 In response to complaints, the town imposed a speed limit forbidding "driving of horses in the streets of the town at a rate of speed inconsistent with public safety." Anyone riding through the streets on horseback or in a carriage, open or closed (no loopholes here), faster than six miles per hour would pay a fine of one dollar for each violation. Clearly, excessive speeds are not only a modern scourge. Less clear is exactly how the speed of a horse was measured by law-enforcement officials in 1807.

Jacob Perkins, inventor

ℰↃ

I n a lifetime that spanned over four-score years, Jacob Perkins applied for and received forty patents. His inventions included nail-making machines, steel engraving plates, pumps, improvements in waterwheels and steam engines, and navigational instruments. Yet few have ever heard of him.

Twelve-year-old Jacob began his career as an apprentice to a goldsmith. Who knows what ideas germinated in young Jacob's mind as he worked making gold-bead necklaces? By the early 1790s, the results of his ingenuity began to appear. First he designed a machine for minting coins. Next he created a machine for cutting and heading nails in one operation, and this he put to commercial use. With two partners, he started his business in a shop in Byfield and later moved it to Amesbury.

Jacob Perkins was an inventor above all else, so once an invention was operational, he lost interest and moved on, using profits from the established business to fund new experiments. This pattern, which repeated throughout his career, caused friction with his business partners, and before the eighteenth century ended, the first partnership fell apart, leaving Perkins with nothing to show for his work. He even had to relinquish his patents to his partners.

Perkins probably didn't fret for long, however, busy as he was perfecting his stereotype steel plate for printing banknotes. Prior to Perkins's innovation, individual banks printed their own currency using copper plates. This, unfortunately, allowed for easy counterfeiting.

Perkins's system was dramatically different. He engraved up to sixty-four small separate dies with intricate designs, letters, and figures. These were clamped together in a strong frame, forming one die. This design was transferred onto a metal plate, which in turn printed the paper. Later, Perkins would find a way to harden the steel so the plates wouldn't wear out so fast. His invention revolutionized the printing of money, and forgery was dramatically reduced though not eliminated. Until well after 1825, in a workshop on Fruit Street, Jacob's brother Abraham ran a business that printed almost all the money used by banks in Maine, New Hampshire, and Massachusetts.

Even though Jacob Perkins moved on to other inventions, patenting twelve of them between 1810 and 1815, his steel-plate printing method remained a constant in his life. It also accounted for his leaving Newburyport. In 1816, he moved to Philadelphia, hoping the new Second Bank of the United States would adopt his invention. It did, but the bank failed shortly thereafter.

Three years later, Perkins, at age fifty-three, sailed to England. The Bank of England had been experiencing the same difficulties with counterfeiting as had banks in the United States, and Perkins hoped to make it a convert, too. He failed, but the Bank of Ireland did contract for his steel engraving plates, and Perkins's newly created company received more than enough business from city and county banks. The firm of Perkins, Bacon, & Petch remained in business (with changes in the name) until 1935.

Despite the success of his banknote engraving business in

Newburyport, Perkins, his mind occupied with other matters, incurred significant debt during his time in Philadelphia. It was not until 1834 that his brother finally managed to settle Jacob's debts with about twenty-five creditors. And in London, the pattern repeated itself.

Perkins became increasingly interested in improving steam engines, and once again he siphoned money away from his company to fund expensive experiments. Though his name remained with the company, his partnership, and hence any profit-sharing, ended.

A few years before Perkins's death, his steel-plate engraving invention once again made news. In 1840, the British government awarded Perkins, Bacon, & Petch the contract for printing the first penny postage stamps in Great Britain. The company would print 22 billion stamps for Britain and the Empire before Perkins's method would be replaced.

Perhaps if Jacob Perkins had rested on his laurels and accumulated huge profits from his steel-plate engraving invention, he would be remembered by more people today. But then he wouldn't have been the same Jacob Perkins.

Embargoed

The Embargo Act of 1807, which prohibited ships from leaving for foreign ports, infuriated many New Englanders, especially those whose livelihood depended on the sea. Shipping came to an abrupt halt, prompting the *Newburyport Herald* to write, "Our wharves have now the stillness of the grave,—indeed nothing flourishes on them but vegetation." The ban suffocated the town's economy. Townspeople sent a petition to President Thomas Jefferson asking for a change in policy, but Jefferson, hoping to avoid war by placing economic pressure on the French and British, left the embargo in place.

A "traveling preacher" sold for only fifty cents, while a statue believed to be William Pitt fetched one dollar.

Newburyport observed the first anniversary of the act by ringing church bells and firing guns—signals usually reserved for notifying citizens of disaster. Flags flew at half-mast, and sailors marched to the sound of funereal drums, wearing black draped over their arms. On a horse-drawn cart lay pieces of a ship. The banner above read "Death to Commerce."

Finally, in 1810, Congress lifted all restrictions to international shipping and Newburyport's economy began to revive.

Pitt, two arms, and a hand

What became of the forty-plus statues from Lord Timothy Dexter's museum? Newburyport legends offer a multiple choice:

A. All were taken away and smashed into pieces so they could never be sold.

B. They were "consigned to their proper place—the flames" (according to historian Mrs. E. Vale Smith).

C. They were sold at auction.

D. All of the above.

Six months after Timothy Dexter's death, in 1806, the *Newburyport Herald* advertised a public auction of his lordship's statues. Most remained in place at 201 High Street, however, to be felled by the hurricane of 1815. Finally, another auction disposed of the last of the illustrious wooden personages for next to nothing. A "traveling preacher" sold for only fifty cents, while a statue believed to be William Pitt fetched one dollar. Perhaps at this point someone bought the rest, broke them further, and eventually burned them.

Two arms and a hand found shelter with Lydia and Maria Currier, who in 1914 donated them to the Historical Society of Old Newbury. Fortunately, Prime Minister Pitt became the possession of the Little family in Brookline, Massachusetts. In 1949 he was given to the Smithsonian Institution. There the tired statue underwent extensive restoration but was never placed on public display.

Twentieth-century Newburyporters, who apparently felt more kindly toward the late Lord Timothy's eccentricities, got wind of the statue's presence in the nation's capital. In 1994, the Historical Society asked to borrow Pitt to be part of a temporary exhibit. Three years later the society approached the Smithsonian once again, this time requesting a permanent loan. The statue now stands on the second floor of the Cushing House Museum for all to admire. One of the unidentified arms rests alongside.

The Great Fire

✿

The moon rose over the town of Newburyport, its light replacing the lingering pastels of a late spring sunset. But the night of May 31, 1811, was not destined to be remembered for its serene beginning. Around 9:00 P.M. from the heart of town, just a few yards from Market Square, came the dreaded cry "Fire!"

People responded instantly. Some raced to the churches where minutes later all the bells began to ring. Others grabbed their leather fire buckets. As soon as they heard the bells sounding the alarm, scores of volunteer firefighters from the six companies in town hastened first to the churches to find out where to go, then to their fire stations to pull the fire-fighting equipment to the scene.

By the time they arrived at the stable on Inn Street, where the fire had begun, it was completely engulfed in flames. The men's job was to contain the fire; rarely could buildings where fires began be saved.

Quickly they unrolled the hoses from the reels and attached them to the front of the handtub, a wagon with a large water-holding tank. Townspeople formed two lines reaching down to the river. On one side men passed full buckets up to the handtub, while opposite them women and children handed empty ones back down. Firefighters, eight to ten on each side, pumped the railings on the sides of the handtub, forcing the water out the hoses. Every five or ten minutes the pumpers were spelled because the work was so exhausting.

Everyone battled frantically, but in vain. Weeks of dry weather had preceded this final night in May. Now strong westerly winds spread the blaze through wooden buildings packed close together. Stables filled with hay erupted, roaring. Sparks flew through the air. Sheets of flame rose skyward. At one point they met in an arch across State Street. One after another, homes collapsed in upon themselves. Thick smoke tinged with a lurid orange obliterated the night sky. Incredibly, people from as far away as Attleboro, Massachusetts, and Amherst, New Hampshire, reported seeing the glow of the fire. Closer by, residents of Amesbury, Newbury, Ipswich, Rowley, Salisbury, Beverly, and Topsfield were among the many who either saw or heard of the disaster and came to offer assistance.

The fire raged on, part way up State Street, but mainly east, consuming everything in its path out to Fair Street and down to the wharves on Water Street. Those who weren't involved in fighting the inferno clogged the streets, running from the suffocating heat, moving possessions from their homes and businesses to locations presumed safe. One such destination was the Baptist Church on Liberty Street, but before the night was over, that too burned, taking with it all its contents.

At two in the morning, the desperate residents of Newburyport thought they were about to lose the whole town. They tore down several buildings in the fire's path in one more attempt to stop its spread. But thankfully around four o'clock the wind must have reversed itself, and with nothing left to consume, the fire began to die out.

Sixteen and a half acres of the most densely built area of town lay smoldering in piles of charred beams and ashes. Two hundred and fifty buildings, including ninety homes—gone.

Everyone battled frantically, but in vain. Weeks of dry weather had preceded this final night in May. Now strong westerly winds spread the blaze through wooden buildings packed close together.

Almost all the dry goods stores—gone. Four printing offices—gone. The Custom House—gone. Four bookstores, four attorneys' offices, the post office—all gone. Seven wharves—gone. Total losses were estimated at $1 million.

Four days later, Sarah Anna Emery walked among the ruins and later wrote, "It was indescribably sad to see the large space covered with charred debris and half-fallen chimneys . . . [It was] such a vivid picture of household desolation that I turned hastily away and left the scene."

Naturally, Newburyporters offered shelter and help to the hundreds of homeless. Donations came from beyond as well, totaling $128,000. Boston sent $24,000. From Salem came $10,000. Philadelphia sent $13,000. From Enfield and Canterbury, New Hampshire, Shakers drove to the decimated town bringing five cartloads of furniture, food, and clothing.

Shortly afterward, the state legislature passed an act in hopes of preventing such a disaster in the future. A set of regulations dictated that buildings between Market Square and Federal Street be built of brick or stone. Extended firewalls rising between the buildings are clearly visible today. In addition, no wooden buildings more than twenty-five feet high were permitted anywhere in town. Within a month, men cleared the debris and laid foundations. Before winter gripped the town, many dry goods and grocery stores opened for business, and a year later, Mrs. Emery remarked that the town looked better than before. Recovery slowed after this, however, as the War of 1812 once again halted commerce, and many years dragged by before all physical traces of the fire had disappeared.

Fear lingered in town. From the beginning, many suspected that an arsonist was behind the horrific conflagration, since several quickly contained fires had begun in the same location earlier that spring. But no culprit was ever found.

Newburyporters would remember the kindness of strangers. Just two years later, over eighty men rushed to Portsmouth, New Hampshire, to help guard property and extinguish the flames of a giant fire. In decades to come, to those ravaged by fire in Maine, Virginia, North and South Carolina, and closer to home in Gloucester and on Nantucket Island, the people of Newburyport sent money and necessities to offset losses.

Given time, he spoke in rhyme

Enoch Toppan approached town perched on a tired old wagon pulled by an equally tired white horse. The store owner watched him draw near and then turned to the stranger who had asked directions. "Ask that man," he said, pointing to Mr. Toppan. "If he doesn't answer you in rhyme, I will give you a glass of gin." The stranger turned to the rhymester and repeated his question.

"If the distance was but little shorter, I should say 'twas a mile and a quarter," Mr. Toppan answered quickly, and then he turned to the store owner with a grin. "When next you promise gin," he said, "speak low or you'll get taken in."

When his business of making blocks for ships' rigging slowed, and especially after his workshop on the wharf burned down in the Great Fire, Enoch Toppan took to the local roads. Sometimes he sang, other times he played his violin, almost always he spoke in rhyme. Few could resist the cheerful, amiable man, and they rewarded him for the light he brought to their days by giving him odd jobs.

Captain William Nichols

As a child William Nichols of Newburyport must surely have been incorrigible, for as an adult he drove the British navy crazy. His adventures with them began in 1811. The English and French had been battling (again), and Nichols, in command of the brig *Alert* with a cargo of brandy, wines, and silk, ran the British blockade near Bordeaux. The following day a frigate captured him, took all of his men but four, and ordered the *Alert* to Plymouth with an English prize crew on board. Nichols retook his ship shortly after midnight and sent the English off in boats to reach safety on the coast of France as best they could.

Unfortunately for Nichols, another British frigate stopped him a week later and took the Americans prisoner. But upon reaching shore, Nichols thwarted them once more. He escaped and returned home.

Within a year, the United States declared war on England, in part as a result of the kind of interference with international commerce experienced by Nichols. The War of 1812 was hugely unpopular in Newburyport. Men would rather have chanced the occasional loss of a ship than have the sea trade cease completely. Unlike in the Revolutionary War, when patriotism played a part in privateering, most who engaged in capturing enemy ships this time did so purely for economic survival.

On August 4, 1812, Captain Nichols sailed out of Newburyport on the brig *Decatur* armed with fourteen guns and manned by 160 men. In less than two months he returned having captured one bark, seven brigs, and one ship. He brought back fifty-four prisoners and cargoes that included salt, coal, fish, sugar, and rum. Then he went off again to capture three more vessels.

His key to success was simple. He would order his best marksman to "keep the helm of the enemy clear." In one confrontation, his crewman shot four English sailors who tried to take the wheel, but for the most part no one dared to try after the first man fell. The enemy ship, unable to maintain its heading, would be vulnerable to capture.

Despite his clever tactics, Nichols was not totally invincible, and the British *Surprise* captured the *Decatur* after a prolonged conflict and took Nichols to Barbados. To our hero's utter dismay, who should recognize him in port but the English captain of the frigate that had captured him before war broke out! The captain promptly confined Nichols on the quarter-deck in a seven-by-five-foot cage. For thirty-four days his only human contact was one guard.

Finally the British sent Nichols to prison in England where they threatened to hang him. Nichols's lucky streak was not over yet, however. United States officials were holding two English officers as hostages, and the captain remained unharmed for ten months until the two sides arranged a prisoner swap.

Nichols returned to Newburyport and six weeks later took command of the brig *Harpy* and her crew of one hundred men. "The Holy Terror," as the English had nicknamed him, was at it again! One after another, he captured English vessels until, by war's end, he had taken twenty-eight prizes.

Among the last ships he captured, less than a month before hostilities ended, was the *William and Alfred,* which was sailing from London to Antigua. Her captain wrote a grateful testimonial commending Captain Nichols and all his officers "for their great civility, indulgent lenity and humane usage while on board" and invited the captain and officers to visit him at his home in London. Four other shipmasters of vessels taken by the *Harpy* not only supported the testimonial, but went on to express their desire "that such humanity and goodness may be made public, as well in the United States as in England" and to "declare that our treatment is worthy of every praise and encomium." These were noteworthy commendations, indeed, in light of Nichols's experiences as an English prisoner.

Meanwhile back home, opposition to the war intensified. In January 1815 a group of Newburyport citizens, with Ebenezer Moseley as their moderator, sent a letter to the Massachusetts legislature suggesting "that the laws of the United States shall be temporarily suspended in their operation in our territory, and that hostilities shall cease towards Great Britain on the part of the free, sovereign and independent states of New England." Fortunately, the letter had no ill consequences, because in

February 1815 news reached town of a peace treaty between the two countries. Townspeople rejoiced by firing cannons and ringing church bells.

Captain Nichols continued to sail the seas for more than a decade until he bought a house on Harris Street and settled down to life as a merchant. Several times Newburyporters elected him to town office, and for four years he served as collector of customs under President Polk. Captain William Nichols died on February 12, 1863, and lies buried in Oak Hill Cemetery.

Square-riggers

Federalist mansions are known locally as "square-riggers." The name pays tribute to the captains who sailed three-masted, square-rigged ships and returned home to build square, three-storied mansions.

Highway robbery

In the early 1800s, robbery was a capital offense. After news spread of the crime committed against Major Elijah P. Goodridge, many found comfort in the fact that after capture the villains would surely hang.

Around ten o'clock on the night of December 19, 1816, Major Goodridge stumbled to the toll house near Pearson's Tavern on the Essex-Merrimack Chain Bridge. Clothes soiled, hatless, his left hand sticky with blood, he spoke incoherently: Men . . . Three men . . . Attacked by three men . . . Beaten on head. Wounded hand . . . They dragged him over fence, into a field, stabbed, and robbed him . . . Hundreds of dollars . . . Three men . . . Beaten unconscious . . .

The appalled innkeeper led the major to his tavern and sent for a doctor. The victim rambled on and asked for people to search for his horse and belongings. Several ventured forth with lanterns and found many items, including a pistol, a billfold, and a bloodied whip. They recovered $36 of the $1086 in banknotes the major had been carrying with him, but none of the $669 in gold.

As the doctor examined him, Major Goodridge moaned, complaining of severe pains in his side and on the back of his head. He remained somewhat delirious for three days, then gradually regained his health.

Five days after the crime, the *Newburyport Herald* wrote that the "high-handed and daring offence surpasses in boldness of action as well as wickedness of deed anything before known and now recollected in this vicinity." The townspeople shuddered in horror, for on the same night, someone had also tried to break into a store on Cornhill. To the $300 reward offered by the victim, they added $700 of their own. No one dared to go out at night unarmed.

In just a few days, the authorities arrested seventy-year-old Ebenezer Pearson, the innkeeper, because the wrappers in which the gold was held were found near his tavern. For lack of further evidence, however, he was soon released.

A week later, Major Goodridge arrived with a "wizard" who intended to use his divining rod to find where the robbers had buried the money. A number of people scoffed at such medieval tactics, but the small, stooped man proceeded to search, witch-hazel stick in hand. The end of this magical rod was wrapped in leather that had been dipped in the ashes of a witch. He came up with dirty and torn papers tied in a bundle in the tavern's privy and six pieces of gold in back of the building. Once again, Mr. Pearson was arrested, but to the relief of many townspeople who held the elderly innkeeper in high regard, he was again let go.

Suspicion now shifted to two brothers by the name of Kenniston and a third man, Taber. Major Goodridge accompanied the deputy sheriff in the search of the Kenniston house and there found some incriminating evidence. But Taber had an iron-clad alibi: he had been in jail on the night of December 19. The Kennistons' alibis, though, were shaky, and in April 1817 their trial began. Troubling questions arose about whether Goodridge might have planted evidence as he "searched" the Kenniston house. The doctor who had examined the victim testified that he had seen no wounds on his head or side. Furthermore, he believed that the major was "not deranged but playing the crazy man." He had insisted he couldn't move, but when he thought the doctor couldn't see him, he climbed out of bed and straightened his hair. The jury returned a verdict of not guilty.

Six months later yet another individual, Joseph Jackman, was accused and brought to trial. His case ended in a hung jury. Whispers about Goodridge's truthfulness now were audible. In April 1818, when Mr. Jackman stood trial again, many adamantly argued that the robbery was a sham. But Major Goodridge still had friends who could not imagine someone with his fine reputation doing such a thing.

At the final trial, much of the evidence was the same. Daniel Webster, one of the three attorneys for the defense, presented an eloquent closing argument. He questioned how Goodridge could have been knocked unconscious, fallen from his horse onto frozen ground, and been dragged over a fence and beaten, without a scratch or a bruise on him. He asked what proof existed that Major Goodridge ever had any of the money he claimed he had carried with him. In summary, the robbery had never happened!

All but one member of the jury agreed. The sole juror voting guilty was intractable. As deliberations dragged on, one juror lit a cigar. When the others saw that the holdout found cigar smoke distasteful, without a word being said, eleven men soon sat puffing. The smoke grew so dense that many became teary-eyed, and finally the twelfth juror acquiesced.

Major Elijah P. Goodridge was never seen again; word was he went south. Apparently he had been in severe financial difficulty and staged the robbery to divert attention from his debts. Immediately after the verdict his effigy was hung from a makeshift gallows erected on the hill where he claimed to have been so viciously attacked.

Beggars' Night

Beggars' Night lasted three nights, beginning on the Monday before Thanksgiving. Primarily women and children came knocking on back doors. Elizabeth Little Coffin remembers standing in the shadows as a child and watching her grandmother and mother invite the "beggars" in to sit and warm themselves by the hearth. They passed out food such as cooked potatoes or cornmeal. Katherine Dodge writes of her Grandmother Storey giving out turkeys, chickens, and legs of lamb. By the end of the nineteenth century, this custom disappeared, to be replaced by a night when young boys were apt to get into mischief. Residents recall that in the 1920s and 1930s Beggars' Night took place on Halloween, with candy as the handout. It was also known as Cabbage Stump Night because disappointed youth would throw cabbage stumps at doors that remained shut.

Bumblebee Titcomb

Mr. Titcomb, a carpenter by trade, was displeased when a bumblebee landed near his hand. Apparently he was a man who believed in a rapid and overwhelming response to a perceived threat, because he raised his hatchet declaring, "Now, old fellow, your end has come! Say your prayers, for death is nigh. One, two, three—strike!" Down came the hatchet, cutting off the end of Mr. Titcomb's thumb. The startled bee flew up and stung him on his nose. For ever after, the carpenter was known in town as Bumblebee Titcomb.

Fishermen's tale

Skipper Tarbell had fished the waters of Massachusetts Bay as far back as his memory could drift, and he recognized a fair autumn day when he felt one. With his two sons, ages eighteen and sixteen, he confidently sailed his pinkie, a two-masted fishing boat known for its high, narrow stern, out to Cashes Ledge. Seventy miles from Newburyport, the men cast line after line into the sea, and they soon had a boatload of halibut and cod.

As they were readying to sail home, the wind died down. Patiently they awaited its return. Day slipped into night, and still only the currents kept their boat in motion. Later at night, the father saw a breeze rippling across the surface toward them, but a careful look about brought less welcome news. Dark clouds marked the east, clouds that seemed to spread across the sky even as he watched.

Quickly, father and sons set the sails and prepared to run before the wind. They needed to get away from the rocky shoals, so fine for fishing but treacherous for boats in a storm. Perhaps with luck, they might reach the shore before the full force of wild weather reached them.

Tarbell continued to scud as long as he could, letting the wind at his back drive them to safety, but when he saw a squall fast approaching, he knew he had to reef his sails, and he called to his sons to lower them.

They worked as fast as the wind permitted, straining to control the flapping canvas, but before they could secure the sails, the storm was upon them. Wind lashed the sails against the rigging, stays, masts. Before their horrified eyes, it reduced the canvas to tatters. The sea rose around them, and the skipper turned his back to the shore and pointed his vessel into the wind. Without any sails up, though, he could not keep her steady. Wind and waves twisted her at will.

At times when the fishing boat managed to ride the towering waves around her, her small size seemed an advantage. But when sheets of spray lifted off the tops of breakers and engulfed the vessel all the way to the top of her masts, the men feared that neither they nor the pinkie would ever crest another wave again.

The storm raged through the day, father and sons powerless to alter their fate. With each passing hour, they blew closer to land, but since they could no longer steer, land now presented itself as a danger rather than a salvation. Wind or waves or both would toss their boat onto rocks with no more effort than it took for a man to flip a piece of driftwood away.

In one last desperate attempt at slowing their passage toward the coastline, the skipper cut down his masts, leaving nothing above the hull for the wind to propel. Then father and sons retreated to the cuddy to pray.

A little after midnight, their vessel tossed ever more wildly. From the increased roar of the breakers, the men concluded that land lay close by. They stripped and prepared to plunge into the ocean, calculating that whatever slim chance of survival remained, it would be greater if they swam than if they stayed with the boat as it smashed ashore.

Whatever sense the father relied on, it was not sight, for they could make out nothing. But more than once, he kept his boys from leaping into the sea. Then suddenly the water around them was calm, even though the storm had in no way abated. The skipper lowered his hand-lead overboard. The weight sank to the bottom, and the markings on the line told him that they floated in just thirty feet of water. Immediately they threw out both anchors. The anchors caught, and for the first time their pinkie rested quietly. The men had no idea where they might be.

Dawn brought little relief from the gale, but through the driving rain, father and sons looked toward a town. Steeples rose

above roofs, and wharves reached out toward the sea—
Newburyport! Miraculously, wind and waves had lifted them
over the sandbar at the mouth of the Merrimack River and into
sheltered waters. They settled down to wait for the storm to
spend itself and for help to arrive.

The hanging of Stephen Clark

ℰℛℷ

The seventeen-year-old defendant stood before the court in
Salem as Chief Justice Parker pronounced the sentence. Having
been found guilty of arson, Stephen Merrill Clark of
Newburyport would "be hanged by the neck till he be dead."

Even though many capital offenses existed on the books in
the early nineteenth century, executions were uncommon. In the
thirty years preceding Clark's case, an average of six people a
decade had been hung in Massachusetts, and in the
Commonwealth's history dating back to 1652, when arson
became a capital crime, only a handful of those convicted of setting fire to a dwelling had been sentenced to death.

From beginning to end, Stephen Clark's case lasted less than
a year. At 10:00 P.M. on May 18, 1820, a barn filled with hay
burned to the ground on Green Street in Newburyport. Citizens
suspected arson. Just three days later, cries of "fire" rang through
the streets once again. This time a stable on Temple Street crum-
pled in flames. As the fire raged, two adjoining stables went
down with it, followed by a two-family home and a large single-
family home. Firefighters tore down a third home and a barn to
preserve other buildings and thus managed to contain the blaze.
No one doubted that an arsonist lurked in their midst.

Stephen Clark already sported a reputation as a loudmouth.
At fourteen he had been fined by a magistrate for assault and bat-
tery of an old man. He had failed at two apprenticeships. His
father was at a loss, because, to make matters worse, his son had

become involved with "an abandoned woman," one Hannah Downes. Before the fire, the father had approached the selectmen to seek help for his unruly son.

Shortly after the conflagration, authorities arrested Clark, but because no evidence existed tying him to the suspected arson, he was soon released. During his short stay in jail, his cell abutted that of Hannah Downes and a friends of hers. The two women were awaiting hearings as "persons of lascivious behaviour."

Within weeks, Clark was arrested again and charged with arson. He vehemently denied any involvement. Then the magistrate told him he had been betrayed by Hannah Downes. At this point, according to the magistrate's later testimony, Clark confessed his guilt even though authorities had warned him that a confession could be used as evidence against him.

His trial began on February 15, 1821. The state charged Stephen Merrill Clark with the capital crime of arson—willful and malicious burning of a dwelling or of any other building that resulted in the burning of a dwelling between sunset and sunrise. The twelve-man jury sat listening to the testimony. Not a single juror came from Newburyport.

The prosecutor's case was straightforward. Clark, he stated, confessed twice, first to Hannah Downes and then to Magistrate Woart and the selectmen of Newburyport. Hannah Downes testified that Clark had described to her in great detail, which she related to the court, how he had set the fire in the stable's loft.

The defense attorney countered by asserting that no direct evidence linked Stephen Clark to the crime and that the confession to Hannah Downes should be discounted because it was made to a "person of infamous character." The one to the magistrate was made under "undue influence." Furthermore, Stephen Clark had an alibi. The defense attorney also noted that all the witnesses for the prosecution were from Newburyport and that their testimony should be weighed in light of the town's recent tragic experience with fire.

The defense attacked Hannah Downes unmercifully, calling several people to the stand who testified to her "loose" character and general untrustworthiness. Clark's sisters, cousin, and father insisted that, with the exception of five to ten minutes around nine o'clock, the youth had been with one of them.

After a two-day trial the jury deliberated for four and a half hours. Their verdict: guilty. Even though the jury unanimously supported a commutation of the sentence, the governor's council turned down the appeal, citing their "regard to the safety of the community." Letters from citizens for and against Clark's hanging appeared in newspapers throughout Essex County. Two days before his execution, two men were charged with bringing the youth tools to aid his escape. All efforts to change Clark's destiny had failed.

Huge crowds came to witness Stephen Clark's final passage through Salem out to Winter Island in Salem Harbor, where the gallows stood. One contemporary account estimates the crowd at ten thousand. While newspapers wrote of Clark's resigned and contrite demeanor, sixteen years later a legislative committee debating the abolition of the death penalty heard a dramatically different version: "Such was his horror of death, that it was found necessary, amidst his cries and lamentations, actually to force him from his cell, and drag him to the place of execution."

At 2:00 P.M. on May 10, 1821, the Commonwealth of Massachusetts executed Stephen Merrill Clark. Thirty-one years later, arson, along with a number of other crimes, ceased to be a capital offense.

Travel overland

ᗒᗷ

In 1801 for $2.50 travelers could take a stagecoach from Newburyport at 7:00 A.M. and arrive in Boston at 4:00 P.M. Subsequent years brought improvements in transportation until in 1818 owners of several stage lines incorporated as the Eastern Stage Company. Newburyport craftsmen built all the coaches, including the first ones in the country to be mounted on springs.

Stages took passengers to destinations such as Lowell and Boston, as well as to Hampton, Dover, and Exeter, New Hampshire. They also provided connections with other companies in New England and New York. In 1825, the company owned 35 coaches, 12 chaises, and 287 horses and employed 500 men. In addition, they held large interests in hotels and taverns along their routes. But by the mid-1830s competition from other coaches began to cut into profits, and when the decade ended, train service laid the company to rest.

Train service between Newburyport and Boston was instituted in June 1840. Travelers had the choice of leaving the port at 7:30, 10:00, or 4:00, and returning trains departed Boston at 7:00, noon, and 3:30. Twenty-five years later, competition among three companies brought the fare down to fifty cents. Meanwhile trains also ran from Newburyport to Danvers via Georgetown, Boxford, and Wenham, as well as to Amesbury and Salisbury.

After April 1, 1976, weeds began to choke the railbed to the state capital. No trains ran from Newburyport until late October 1998, when service to Boston resumed.

The Chain Bridge collapse

The day in early February 1827 bristled with cold. David Jackman and Frederick Carlton sat on their cart, huddled deep in their overcoats, a blanket across their legs, hats pulled low. Four oxen and a horse pulled them through deep snow, heading north toward the Essex-Merrimack Chain Bridge. Built in 1810, this suspension bridge spanned 220 feet between Newburyport and Deer Island.

The team lumbered forth. Just as they neared the midpoint of the bridge, chains snapped. In rapid succession, five of the ten chains broke in different places and the bridge collapsed. Cart, animals, and men plunged forty feet into the frigid waters of the Merrimack River.

Thrashing desperately, Jackman and Carlton struggled up for air. Sections of the bridge, which had come crashing down as well, floated around them. The men grabbed hold of pieces of timber. Materials that seconds earlier could have killed them now kept them afloat.

So cold that their teeth chattered uncontrollably, the men battled the current. Their wool coats and water-filled boots weighed them down as they slowly swam toward land, where half an hour later onlookers pulled them out. They wrapped the men in thick, dry blankets and drove them home as rapidly as road conditions would allow. Jackman, the older of the two men, took longer to recover from the extreme exposure. Otherwise, both were unhurt.

Remarkably, the horse survived, too. The oxen, however, did not. Tangled together in their traces, they were swept downstream and trapped beneath ice, where they drowned.

Hundreds of people made their way to view the wreckage, which the *Newburyport Herald* described as "crushed and broken timbers suspended by messy chains [hanging] lazily from pyramidical abutments."

In rapid succession, five of the ten chains broke in different places and the bridge collapsed. Cart, animals, and men plunged forty feet into the frigid waters of the Merrimack River.

Since the Essex-Merrimack bridge was one of the first chain bridges built in this country, its collapse gave special cause for concern. The breakage was initially attributed to the extreme cold and the excessive weight of deep snow. Later, however, questions arose about defects in the chains.

The bridge was privately owned. Shareholders immediately reassured travelers that their plans would not be disrupted by the accident. The ice was thick enough all across the river just west of the bridge to provide safe passage. Heavier loads would be transported by boat. Messrs. Jackman and Carlton were reimbursed for all losses. By the end of the month, the owners had met, estimated repair costs at $4,000, and made plans to repair the bridge. It reopened for traffic on July 17, 1827, and carried all who used it safely across until it was taken over by the county and rebuilt in 1909.

Travel up river and along coast

Steamers traveled up the Merrimack from Newburyport to Haverhill beginning in 1828. They also took passengers to the Isles of Shoals, Portsmouth, and, of course, Boston. The business first began by offering occasional excursions in the summer, but twenty years later steamers ran between Newburyport and Boston twice a week. Even after trains and, later, streetcars dominated travel, summer service to Haverhill continued, until the early years of the twentieth century.

William Lloyd Garrison

The statue of abolitionist William Lloyd Garrison in Brown Square belies the contentious relationship he had with the town where he was born. His childhood years in Newburyport were short and troubled. When Garrison was just three, his alcoholic father abandoned the family. A few years later, his mother, hoping to find work in the shoe industry, moved to Lynn, taking her daughter with her but leaving her two sons with separate families. Young William had to drop out of school to work, ran away once, and at age nine began a short-lived apprenticeship at a shoemaker's. An apprenticeship as cabinetmaker failed also. It wasn't until 1818, when he was thirteen, that he experienced stability in his life, when he joined the *Newburyport Herald* for his third and final apprenticeship, this time as a printer.

In 1829 Garrison moved to Baltimore, having taken up the cause of two million enslaved African-Americans. Together with a partner, he published an abolitionist paper, *Genius of Universal Emancipation.*

Though the transatlantic slave trade had ended in 1808, slaves were routinely transported along the American coast from city to city. Garrison grew angry when he saw that many northern vessels participated in this coastal trade, and he chose the *Francis,* owned by Francis Todd of Newburyport, as his example.

In November 1829 he wrote in *Genius* that the *Francis* had sailed with seventy-five slaves from New Orleans to Baltimore. The next week, he increased his attacks on Todd. The shipowner's name appeared in bold print throughout, and Garrison, employing strong language, noted that it was quite clear that Todd made large profits solely by transporting slaves. He then sent the article to Francis Todd.

Todd filed suit for libel, claiming $5,000 in damages. A grand jury in Baltimore promptly followed by indicting Garrison for "a gross and malicious libel against Francis Todd and Captain Nicholas Brown"—a criminal charge.

Six weeks later, William Lloyd Garrison was tried by jury and found guilty of criminal libel. The judge fined him fifty dollars and another fifty dollars in court costs. Unable to raise such a sum, Garrison was confined to jail on April 17, 1830.

Garrison, like many activists who came before and after him, welcomed the libel charge and subsequent jail time as publicity for his cause. Denied neither paper nor ink, he spent his time writing to, among others, Todd, the presiding judge, the prosecutor, and the agent who arranged the transportation of slaves.

A pamphlet he wrote in which he denounced the trial as "a mockery of justice" caught the attention of Arthur Tappan of New York, who sent the money to pay Garrison's fine and gain his release. After seven weeks, Garrison walked free once more.

He returned north to Boston, letting Todd's civil suit succeed by default. The case was tried without the defendant, and the jury awarded Francis Todd $1,000, but the shipowner never exacted payment of the damages.

Garrison sought to spread his convictions through public lectures, but he often had difficulty finding a hall. Just a few months after his trials, he asked to speak in Newburyport. His reception was at best mixed. He spoke at the Titcomb Street Church but caused such a commotion that he was asked not to do so again.

In January 1831, together with fellow Newburyport native Isaac Knapp, Garrison published the first issue of the abolitionist journal *The Liberator*. The closing words of his famous editorial read, "I will be heard." Hundreds of people in towns large and small heard William Lloyd Garrison's passionate speeches, but his return to Newburyport in 1832 was marred by refusals once more. It took twenty-five years before the Lyceum Association invited him to speak at City Hall, where a large audience welcomed him. John Lord wrote in his diary, "Only a few years ago he would have been kicked out of the city. . . . Surely the world moves."

The Underground Railroad

M ary Curzon stood still, listening to the rumble of wheels rolling over the dirt. Gradually, out of the darkness, the black shape came into focus. Neither Mary nor her sister ever knew when a wagon might bring a package to remote Curzon Mill, wedged in where the Artichoke River joins the Merrimack. Some came by water, others by land, but either way the deliveries had become routine.

The Quaker hopped off the wagon seat, tipping his hat to the young women, and together they unloaded the packing case. Mary pried open the top, wondering as always who it would be this time—a young man, an older woman, a girl? Would there be a few hours in which the runaway slave could share his story? Would she make it safely to Canada? But the black man inside had nothing to tell them nor a future to draw him. He was dead.

Normally the Curzon sisters hid a fugitive for a day or two in the wine closet of the cellar and later rowed him or her across the river to proceed through hospitable Amesbury. What were they supposed to do with a dead man? Bury him, quickly and quietly. The Quaker got a shovel and dug a grave in the orchard. They read a biblical verse, then replaced the soil and finally the grass on top, as carefully as possible so as not to attract curiosity. To this day, the fugitive with no name lies buried in a grave with no marker.

Men and women, such as the Curzon sisters, took significant risks by participating in the Underground Railroad. Newburyport had more reason than many other communities to oppose the abolitionist movement and turn in someone harboring runaway slaves. By the mid-1840s, four cotton mills operated in town, employing approximately 1,500 people. Cotton mills need cotton, which was picked by slaves. An end to slavery would affect local profits and livelihoods. Not only did William Lloyd Garrison's appearances in Newburyport create controversy, Reverend Thomas Wentworth Higginson resigned from his position as pastor of the Unitarian Church because the wealthier parishioners disapproved of his antislavery activities.

Yet Newburyport lay on one of three trails that took former slaves from Salem north to New Hampshire. Secret activities often pass away with the activists, forgotten save by those whose lives were salvaged. However, several individuals in Newburyport are remembered for their work in helping refugees: Captain Alexander Graves, William Jackman, and Richard Plumer.

A successful dry goods merchant, Plumer lived at 79 Federal Street in a house still standing today. Under cover of dark, he would take his wagon to the bridge over the Parker River where men from Ipswich met him, bringing fugitives. Plumer hid them under sacks of grain and delivered them to the next station. Sometimes he drove to Jackman's property at the north end of town, or to Quaker Robert Brown's farm at Turkey Hill in West Newbury. Other times he took them himself across the Chain Bridge to Amesbury. On occasion, travel was too dangerous, and he hid men and women in his barn or in the cellar under hay. Story has it that some sailed to freedom from Newburyport to Prince Edward Island.

Joshua Coffin, of Newbury, one of the original twelve members of the New England Anti-Slavery Society, not only provided safe refuge at his home on High Road, but at one time he traveled to Tennessee to escort to freedom a free Black man who had been illegally sold into slavery.

Luckily, few fugitives ended their escape the way the man did at Curzon Mill. No one knows how many African-Americans fled the South between 1830 and 1860 with the help of the Underground Railroad, but estimates range in the hundreds of thousands. Scores of those rested in the homes, cellars, and barns of the Newburys before they moved on, heading north to freedom.

First name in silver

ɛ⌐ɔ

In the latter part of the eighteenth century, those who had silver coins to spare often had a silversmith melt them down to transform them into objects such as spoons, tankards, and porringers.

These then served the dual purpose of being useful (a revered New England trait) and more easily recognizable (a deterrent to theft).

The women of the First Religious Society in Newburyport chose to do something a little different with some of their silver dollars. They contributed them toward a gift for the church. A local silversmith melted down the money and reformed it into a baptismal font. Though the bowl bears no mark, it is believed to have been made by one of Newburyport's Moulton silversmiths.

Beginning in the mid-1700s, four generations of Moultons followed the silversmithing profession and may well have the longest family tradition of silvermaking in the country. For a time in the early 1800s, three Moulton firms coexisted in town, which was home to some thirty silversmiths. In 1860 Joseph Moulton sold his business to Anthony Towle (who had once been his apprentice) and William Jones. In the decades to come, their business would evolve into Towle Silversmiths, which had sales around the world.

Descendants of the Moultons gather with friends each year for dinners where the antique silver is used. From the early 1800s through the present day, ministers of the Unitarian First Religious Society have sprinkled water from the silver bowl onto the heads of the church's youngest members during dedication ceremonies.

Shipped home in a cask-et

HAVANA, CUBA—MAY 1841 Two thousand miles from home, Captain Francis Brown Todd lay on the bed, his back and legs savaged by pain, his skin a ghastly yellow. Friend, brother-in-law, and fellow Newburyport captain William Nichols, Jr., sat in a chair next to him, providing comfort by his presence, but helpless to alter the course of yellow fever. The next day, thirty-five-year-old Todd lapsed into a coma, and two days later he died.

Strong ties bound both men to their native city. Each bore his father's name. William Nichols was the son of Captain William Nichols, the "Holy Terror" of the War of 1812, and Francis Brown Todd was the son of Captain Francis Todd who had brought suit against William Lloyd Garrison in 1830.

Nichols made careful arrangements to ship Todd's body home, aware not only of the natural deterioration of the remains, but also of people's fear of the little understood and dreaded disease. He had his friend's body placed in a mahogany coffin encased in one of lead. These were placed inside a massive eighty-gallon oak barrel filled with alcohol and sealed tight. Thus the body of Captain Francis Brown Todd arrived in his hometown where it was buried at New Hill Cemetery.

On the same day that family in Newburyport received word from Captain Nichols describing his friend's illness and death and the shipment of his body home, another letter written by a stranger brought news that Captain Nichols himself had contracted and died from yellow fever within two weeks of his friend's passing. He was twenty-nine.

William Nichols, Sr., sailed to Havana to bring his only son's body back for burial. But young Nichols had had no one to care for him the way he had cared for his friend. He lay buried beneath the cathedral in Havana with many other victims of the disease, his grave unmarked. The bereaved father returned to Newburyport alone.

This tale of friendship and loss has a curious postscript. In 1882, a relative of Captain Todd decided to move his remains to the family lot at Oak Hill Cemetery. Diggers opened the grave at New Hill and found the cask almost as solid as when it was built, its one-inch-thick staves bound tightly by ten three-inch-wide iron hoops. The barrel, with coffins and remains inside and still full of alcohol, was reinterred at Oak Hill, where it has remained undisturbed ever since.

Schooling girls

❦

In 1791, Newburyport's school dames taught girls five to nine years old "proper decency of behavior" and their letters so that they could read any chapter in the Bible. If parents asked for it, their daughters could learn needlework and knitting, as well. A decade later, older girls could attend school, too, for six months of the year from 6:00 A.M. to 8:00 A.M. and on Thursday afternoons. A number of tiny private schools also existed, and they too imparted reading skills together with lessons in embroidery and needlework.

One male teacher at the time allowed his female students to study grammar but, as pupil Sarah Anna Emery reports, would not permit them "to cipher in fractions. . . . It was a waste of time, wholly unnecessary, would never be of the least use. If we could count our beaux and skeins of yarn it was sufficient."

The town's approach to educating women was in keeping with other New England communities and actually in advance of other states and European countries where the widely held belief that women's smaller brains were weaker resulted in their receiving no education at all.

Good fortune came to Newburyport children, especially girls, in the form of Rev. Thomas B. Fox. The newly ordained minister became pastor of the First Religious Society on Pleasant Street in 1831. He brought with him enormous energy and a love of nature and children. With his arrival, church attendance increased dramatically. He added special services just for children, encouraged them to bring in plants and rocks, and organized parish picnics. Fox was definitely not without his critics. His decision to bring fresh flowers into church caused dyed-in-the-wool Puritans to deride the practice as "too terrible to contemplate without a shudder—such Popish folly!"

The minister's commitment to children led him to serve on the school committee, where he is credited with increasing per-pupil spending and dismissing incompetent teachers. In the early 1840s he took on the unprecedented task of establishing a high school for girls. A newspaper article written fifty years later describes his efforts as being "bitterly opposed by the wealthiest citizens . . . who could not tolerate . . . so vulgar a notion as the herding of young women of every grade of society for the purpose of instruction upon matters entirely out of their province." Be that as it may, the school committee presented a highly favorable report to the town meeting, and in March 1843 the men voted to establish what is believed to be the first female high school in the country.

Seventy-eight girls crowded a single room where classes met temporarily while a new building was under construction. The Newburyport Female High School attracted hundreds of visitors from neighboring towns and distant states in its early years, and doubtless improved the lives of many women far beyond city boundaries.

His final act

Martha Wills was engaged to marry Navy officer Wingate Pillsbury. She awaited the return of her fiancé in much the same way as did wives and loved ones of mariners the world over, with resigned patience and anxiety. Above all, she kept herself busy. One hot July day in 1847, when the harbor shimmered in haze, she retreated with her needlework to the summer house behind her family's Federalist home at 77 High Street. The afternoon drifted slowly by. Suddenly Martha heard her fiancé call her name. She leaped to her feet, almost tripping on her needlework, which she had dropped, but he was nowhere to be seen. Inside the house no one knew what she was talking about.

Martha returned to the summer house. She picked up her needle and embroidery hoop, but her hands shook too much to work. She gazed out at the watery image of a nearby maple until hours later it regained its true form.

Weeks elapsed before word reached Newburyport. On the day Martha had heard Wingate call in the garden, he had drowned trying to save the life of a sailor who could not swim. A monument in his honor stands on the grounds of the U.S. Naval Academy in Annapolis. Martha Wills never married. She lived an active life, but died of consumption in her early forties.

The old town house

B rown Street may well be the shortest dead-end street in Newburyport. Until 1937 the road cut through to High Street, but now it primarily gives access to Oak Hill Cemetery. On the left stands a beautifully restored pale yellow house. Like Brown Street, it also used to live a busier life. At one time it served as Newbury's Town House.

A mere thirty years after separating from Newbury, Newburyport began to petition the state government to enlarge its acreage. The town wished chiefly to extend its ownership of waterfront property. In 1846 townspeople considered reuniting with their parent town, but voters defeated that notion at town meeting. In April 1851, the legislature and governor finally approved a transfer of land. Newburyport's size increased from 647 acres to between 6,000 and 7,000 acres (Newbury still had more than twice that acreage), and the town now stretched from the Chain Bridge all along the river past Joppa and across the Plum Island Bridge to include the northern tip of Plum Island. Newburyport's population increased by more than 30 percent.

With the town boundaries redrawn, Newbury's Town House now stood in Newburyport. One month after the changes, Newbury town clerk Joshua Coffin posted the following notice in the *Daily Herald:*

The Annual town meeting of what is left of Newbury stands adjourned to Monday, May 12, 2:00 P.M. at the Town House now in Newbury Port.

Within two years, Newburyport remodeled the building. Fresh paint, green blinds, a steeple, and ornamental woodwork transformed it into Brown High School. In 1868 when Brown High School united with two other high schools and moved opposite Bartlet Mall, the building belonged to private owners for the first time. They moved it off the original foundation and turned it sideways to the street, and so it has remained for over a century, giving little hint of the role it once played.

Wild Boat of the Atlantic

For ten years, the *Dreadnaught,* the most famous of the hundreds of wooden vessels built in Newburyport, flew across the Atlantic as a packet ship on a regular run between New York and Liverpool. Captain Samuel Samuels was so confident of her speed that he guaranteed delivery by certain dates or the freight charge was on him—a practice undertaken by very few skippers. "She was built for hard usage and to make a reputation for herself and me," Samuels said, "and I intended that she should do her duty, or that we both should sink."

While Samuels skippered the *Dreadnaught,* no vessel ever passed her in anything over a four-knot breeze. His average passage, eastbound, lasted a mere nineteen days. In February 1859, the Wild Boat of the Atlantic sped across 3,018 miles of ocean in thirteen days and eight hours. On her best day she traveled 313 miles, and even on her slowest she covered 133. She beat steamers to her destination.

This extraordinary ship, which earned such a reputation at sea, did not reward her creators monetarily. William Currier and James L. Townsend, who designed and built her in 1853, did so

*She washed up on the rocks of Cape Penas, northeast of Tierra del Fuego
in South America. When the captain saw no hope of saving her, he and the
crew lowered the boats.*

at a loss and incurred debts from which they never recovered, closing their shipyard in 1856 while the *Dreadnaught* sailed on.

Samuels was noted for keeping more sails up during a storm than any other captain at sea. But he matched his unequaled drive with fine seamanship skills, and when his ship encountered a furious gale in January 1863, he knew that he and his vessel had best lay low. Only a close-reefed main topsail stayed up, the least amount of canvas possible. Towering waves threatened the 212-foot vessel, and one terrified the men to such a degree that they accidentally turned her the wrong way. Disaster followed. The sea carried away the rudder with its brace, smashed the skylight, and flooded the cabin. Another wave stove in the hatches, and the *Dreadnaught* took on more water. A wave crushed Captain Samuels, fracturing his right leg in several places. As the sea swept over the decks, he was almost lost overboard.

The ocean tossed the ship at will. The captain lay barely conscious in his cabin while a first mate Samuels considered incompetent stood by helplessly. The carpenter had been killed, and panicked passengers added to the chaos. Thankfully, the storm began to abate, and the *Dreadnaught* survived, crippled. The second officer tried to attach a makeshift rudder but failed; the sea was still running too high. On the fifth day after the storm, a passing ship tried all day to turn the vessel around toward the Azores 350 miles away, but could not succeed. Desperately, the next day, Samuels instructed his second officer to sail the *Dreadnaught* backward. It worked, and she covered 183 miles in the next two days. When the wind dropped, once again the crew tried to construct a jury rudder, and this time, in calm seas, they succeeded in attaching it. Fourteen days after the height of the gale, the *Dreadnaught,* with her captain close to death, limped in to Faial, one of the Azores.

Captain Samuels stayed onshore for fifty-two days recovering, and then he boarded the *Dreadnaught* for the last time, sailing for New York. Stateside, he regained his strength slowly. He never resumed command of his beloved ship nor, for that matter, any other sailing vessel. For a short while, he skippered a steamer, but a few years later he gave up the sea altogether. He died in 1908, eighty-five years old.

The *Dreadnaught* meanwhile resumed her run, but 1863 would continue to be a disastrous year for her. In December, she ran into another wild storm. Once again, she lost her rudder. Her shipmaster, Captain Lytle, was so badly injured by a wave that he died a few days later. After the vessel finally returned to New York in late February, she never crossed the Western Sea again.

Yet her sailing days were far from over. The summer of 1864 found her heading for San Francisco. She also made voyages to Honolulu and Australia. In the spring of 1869, she departed Liverpool bound for San Francisco. Twenty-nine days out, she lay becalmed, but unbeknownst to her captain and crew, during the night a strong current carried her close to land. The morning of July 4 dawned to find them among breakers with not a breath of wind to blow the ship to safety. She washed up on the rocks of Cape Penas, northeast of Tierra del Fuego in South America. When the captain saw no hope of saving her, he and the crew lowered the boats.

For seventeen days, they rowed by day and slept on shore at night, scrounging whatever food they could find until a Norwegian bark rescued them near Cape San Diego. Ironically, this flying ship, which had earned her reputation by capturing the wind as few other vessels had, and had survived the worst gales, ended her days forsaken by the wind.

ᏇᎾ

A model of the *Dreadnaught* built by bank teller Henry Currier welcomes visitors today to the Custom House Maritime Museum.

Mansion-turned-library

F ew if any public libraries in the country can claim that President George Washington slept there. Newburyport's can. Did he doze one afternoon while a book lay open on his lap? Well, not quite. When the first president visited Newburyport in October 1789 and spent the night, the building was not yet a library.

In 1771, Patrick Tracy, a wealthy merchant, built the home for his son Nathaniel, who made and lost a fortune in privateering during the Revolutionary War. The Tracy mansion on State Street, which had orchards and gardens extending all the way back to Green Street and was one of *the* show places in town, played host to such notable guests as John Hancock, Thomas Jefferson, John Quincy Adams, and the Marquis de Lafayette.

President George Washington, however, was by far the most illustrious visitor. Two companies of cavalry escorted him to State Street where leading citizens gave the official greeting. The militia punctuated the welcome by firing muskets while fireworks in the evening capped the day. And the president slept in the mansion.

The property changed hands a number of times, serving as the Sun Hotel, a bowling saloon, and a dentist's office. In 1864, it was on the market once again.

Meanwhile, in 1851, the state legislature had passed a law allowing cities and towns to appropriate money for public libraries. Three years later, Josiah Little founded the Newburyport Public Library (one of the first ten public libraries in the Commonwealth and among the first in the country) with a private donation of $5,000. Its collection of 4,000 books lined the shelves of a room in City Hall, but in less than five years, the library outgrew its home. In 1860, members of the Newburyport Lyceum organized a fund-raising campaign for the purchase or construction of a building to house the public library. In addition, Edward S. Moseley, starting with his own donation of $1,000, personally began to solicit contributions, and by 1864 sixty-two donors had contributed $20,273.78.

Six thousand dollars purchased the Tracy mansion, another $10,300 remodeled it, and several thousand dollars were deposited in the bank for future repairs. The property was deeded over to the city, and with its collection of 12,000 books, the library opened to the public in 1866. The original Federalist architecture remains only in the Director's Room and the Reading Room. Intricately carved wood dentil work borders the ceiling, and windows stand recessed behind gracious arches. Throughout the rest of the mansion, beautiful oak carvings from the 1860s draw attention, as do wrought-iron railings lining the balconies.

By the early 1880s, the library needed more space, and the Simpson Annex was built. A century later, the Newburyport Public Library faced challenges once more. Two-hundred-year-old beams built to support a private home could no longer support the weight of over 70,000 books. Floors began to sag. On the second floor balcony, bookcases, once secured between floor and ceiling, separated above, and the iron railing angled forward. Though many temporary solutions kept the library open, more dramatic ones were needed.

In September 1999, the library moved to a barn in the Lord Timothy Dexter Industrial Green while workmen broke ground for a new addition and began restoration of the mansion at a cost of $6.8 million. The new plans called for almost all of the books to be housed in the addition. The eighteenth-century Tracy mansion, besides providing space for tutoring, quiet study, and reference materials, was designated to become home to all of the library's computer technology—so much lighter than books. On the surface this distribution may seem ironic, but it's entirely in keeping with attitudes of the forward-thinking first occupant of the building and the men and women who funded its conversion to a public library.

Launching the *Ontario*

Forget about conducting any business downtown; all the shops were closed. Schoolhouse doors didn't open either on this late September day in 1866. Extra trains came from Boston, Chelsea, and Portsmouth, as well as towns closer by. One boat company advertised trips for twenty-five cents onto the Merrimack River to watch. Everyone flocked to the Jackman shipbuilding yard, where the steamship *Ontario* was about to be launched.

George Jackman, Jr., had built and sent to sea over twenty-five ships, barks, and brigs, but this wooden vessel of 3,000 tons was almost twice the size of anything built on the Merrimack up to that time. Measuring 325 feet long, with a 43-foot beam and three decks, the Ontario was the largest wooden steamship ever built in Massachusetts.

From the beginning, her size had posed many challenges; her launching was the last of these. A launching way was constructed of heavy, wide timbers bolted together to form a track from the bow of a vessel to the low-water mark. The track rested on blocks that were bolted to bed timbers and piles driven through the riverside mud into hard bottom. The art lay in the angle. A launching way had to be steep enough so the ship would slide off smoothly, but not too steep or she might fly off so fast that no one would be able to stop her once she hit water. And the Jackman yard faced an additional problem. It lay opposite Carr's Island, with just a narrow channel between.

The launching was scheduled, as always, for slack tide. A tide that rises an average of nine feet in six hours creates a current that can twist a ship off the way. To avoid that nightmare, shipbuilders waited until a tide was about to turn and the waters of the Merrimack went "slack."

Men had poured hot beef tallow onto the surface of the way until it lay an inch thick. To keep the *Ontario* secured once she hit water, massive ropes rested between the steamer and large apple trees on land. Also her anchors had been buried deep into the mud at water's edge with stakes driven through. Two young men perched on top of the stakes, hoping for the best view in town. Fortunately, they were ordered to move.

Everyone stood ready. Wielding mauls, workers began hammering sharp wedges into the keel blocks, splintering them. The vessel settled onto the greased way and slid, very fast, into the Merrimack. The angle proved to be too steep for a vessel her size.

The ropes tightened instantly, and up went the trees, roots and all, following the steamer straight into the river. Her momentum was so extraordinary that the anchors flew twenty feet into the air and then skittered uselessly along the riverbank. The *Ontario* swept across the narrow channel, and her stern got stuck in the mud off Carr's Island. "A fine launch," noted John Lord in his diary, just exactly what hundreds of people had come to see.

George Jackman was less thrilled. With the help of steam tugs, however, the *Ontario* floated free at the next high tide, and to the shipbuilder's relief, the steamer left Newburyport undamaged to begin her regular run between Boston and Liverpool.

Captain William Wheelwright

✑

Captain William Wheelwright stood staring at the *Rising Empire*, wrecked off the coast of Argentina, a total loss. Wheelwright could have returned to Newburyport carrying depositions describing the events that led to the disaster and taken another command. But the man who took to the sea as a sixteen-year-old cabin boy and rose to shipmaster three years later was not someone who could return home with his tail between his legs. He sent the paperwork but remained in South America, determined to earn back what the ocean had crushed.

Wheelwright made his way around Cape Horn up to bustling Guayaquil, Ecuador (then part of Gran Colombia), where he established a successful trading business and also became the U.S. consul. By 1828 he was ready to pay a visit home, where he married Martha Gerrish. A few weeks later, he sailed with his wife back to South America only to find that his partner had brought their business to the verge of bankruptcy. Wheelwright settled his debts and moved to Valparaiso, Chile.

He would leave his imprint on Chile like no other contemporary. Once again he engaged in coastal trade, but this time by establishing a small line of packet ships which sailed the length of South America's Pacific coast. Within a decade, he began to lay the groundwork for what would become the Pacific Steam Navigation Company (PSNC). With financial backing from Britain, his steamships traveled along the entire coast delivering mail, passengers, and freight to Bolivia, Peru, Ecuador, and Colombia. By the time of Wheelwright's death, PSNC, with sixty ships, was the largest steamship company in the world, having expanded its routes to Europe. Wheelwright's active involvement had ended, however, as soon as the company was up and running.

For Wheelright, it was time to move on. Silver deposits had been discovered in Chile's interior, and as mining began, the need arose for inland transportation. Wheelwright turned his formidable energy to building South America's first railroad of any significant length, and the silver mine owners paid the expenses. In 1850, ten years after the railroad came to his hometown of Newburyport, Wheelwright laid the first section of iron rail in Chile. In a little over a year, a fifty-mile track stretched inland from a new coastal port, and the next year, he began a twenty-six-mile extension. With that project well underway, he took on the challenge of bringing the first gas street lighting to Chile.

Wheelwright was also involved in planning the railroad from Valparaiso to Santiago. He built a piped water supply for

Valparaiso and in his spare time introduced the telegraph to Chile. Wheelwright had Valparaiso and Santiago communicating via telegraph in June 1852, less than five years after the telegraph had been introduced to Newburyport.

Next, Wheelwright pursued his grandest dream, a railroad across the Andes Mountains connecting the Argentinean coast to the Chilean. His efforts to garner support in Chile failed, so the Wheelwrights moved, hoping the Argentineans would be receptive to his idea. They were.

After years of negotiations and planning, Wheelwright's Central Argentinean Railroad Company began construction of a 250-mile track. But Wheelwright would not live to see his dream of a transcontinental railroad fulfilled. In the spring of 1873, he returned to England seeking medical attention, and he died there in September. His body was shipped to his birthplace, where he lies buried in the Oak Hill Cemetery.

Three years after William Wheelwright's death, the citizens of Valparaiso, Chile, raised money for a commemorative statue. Its inscription reads,

> To William Wheelwright
> Citizen of the United States
> From a Grateful People
> Steam Navigation • Railroad • Telegraphs

Not only did William Wheelwright's ventures leave a legacy in South America, the fortune he amassed also left a legacy in Newburyport. The income from two-ninths of his estate was "to be applied to the assistance of such Protestant young men of the city of Newburyport as the said trustees shall consider deserving and meritorious, in obtaining a scientific education."

Since 1882, over 1,500 Newburyport male graduates, locally known as the Wheelwright Boys, have received four-year scholarships toward degrees in the sciences at institutions across the United States, including M.I.T., Harvard, Yale, Amherst, Brown, and Dartmouth. At the end of the twentieth century, the fund was worth over $5 million.

As might be expected, in the 1940s the wording of Wheelwright's will was challenged in court as discriminatory. The suit failed. While all agree that it is discriminatory, it is nonetheless perfectly legal: individuals can will their money to whomever they desire.

William Wheelwright's will was strong indeed. Few natives of Newburyport have had his foresight or impact.

The laurels of Maudslay

Twisted boughs of mountain laurel bushes rise from the woodland floor and reach for light between towering white pines overhead. Hundreds of laurels, one of the largest natural groves in the state, cascade down the slope in Maudslay State Park to the bank of the Merrimack River. In late June, they burst into bloom, covered in clusters of delicate white flowers teased with pink. In 1849, long before the property became a state park, William Ashby chose to hold the first of what would become his famous Laurel Parties right here at the northern tip of Newburyport.

Ashby, an ardent horticulturist, was also active in a number of reform movements, most notably the antislavery campaign. At the first Laurel Party he wedded his two passions by inviting close friends, mainly fellow abolitionists, to join him for a picnic amidst the glorious blossoming laurels. Just one carriage took the group, and in the early years, the parties were informal. A decade later, they had grown significantly larger and taken on a literary theme. Guests came from Boston, Salem, and New Bedford, and included William Lloyd Garrison and Ralph Waldo Emerson. The parties became, in the words of frequent guest John Greenleaf Whittier, the noted poet, "a little too fashionable and conventional for the comfortable lapse into savage freedom that a picnic implies." Yet despite the changes, and even though Whittier usually avoided large groups, the annual Laurel Party remained one of his few public outings.

In 1861, 130 guests arrived, gathering first at the Ashbys' home. Late in the morning, they traveled by carriage, hack, or stage to the laurels where they broke into small groups or couples, wandering the grounds or settling in picturesque spots to chat. At 2:00 P.M. the picnic dinner was served—meats, pies, cakes, jellies, and strawberries. The editor of the *Newburyport Daily Herald* and ex-mayor Albert Currier were among the picnickers who gave speeches. Whittier read his poem "Our River." Then the group sang and finally departed to have tea at Mr. Ashby's.

The party in June 1865 drew the largest crowd. Over three hundred guests came together to celebrate the end of the Civil War and their triumph at abolishing slavery. A steamer with two gondolas attached to the sides carried the joyful group upriver to the laurels once more.

In 1870 the last Laurel Party was held for the reformers and writers who had gathered here over the years, prompting Whittier to write his poem "The Laurels," the fourth stanza of which reads,

> I thank you for sweet summer days,
> For pleasant memories lingering long,
> For joyful meetings, fond delays,
> And ties of friendship woven strong.

At its closure, Ashby collected donations so that poor children in Newburyport could come to their own Laurel Party. William Ashby died in 1881, at age ninety-four. Sadly, nothing seems to grow at his grave in Oak Hill Cemetery.

The laurels, on the other hand, continue to thrive. The Moseley family, who owned adjacent land, added the grove to their property. While renowned landscape architects Charles Sprague Sargent and Martha Brookes Hutcheson supervised the planting of hundreds of rhododendrons and azaleas, dogwoods and hedges throughout the Moseley property, they knew that no human hand could improve on the laurels. In 1985, the state purchased the 476-acre estate, including the laurels, and created Maudslay State Park.

> Make room, O river of our home!
> For other feet in place of ours,
> And in the summers yet to come,
>   Make glad another Feast of Flowers!

Whittier's second-to-last stanza proved prophetic. Every summer, hundreds of visitors picnic here, and concerts and theater productions entertain them in various locations throughout the park. People listen, they laugh, they applaud. And Ashby's vision for art in the gardens lives on.

Ghostly mischief
ℰ↭

The only sounds that broke the quiet in the Charles Street schoolhouse were the edgy shiftings of anticipation. Close to sixty boys sat at desks, their hands moving across slates as they worked on arithmetic problems.

Then the noises they had all been waiting for began again. A knock on the wall. Thumping on the floor so hard their desks shook. The class shivered with fright.

They watched Miss Perkins's face. She didn't speak until her jaw relaxed. "We will recess," she said, and the boys rushed for their coats hanging on hooks in the entryway—but the coats were not there! Once again, they lay in piles on the floor.

Though gloomy in appearance and in need of repairs, everything about the one-room schoolhouse looked normal. Yet nothing was. Since the 1872 school year had begun, students and teachers had been plagued by unexplained pounding, rattling of windows, and eerie voices.

Days passed punctuated by phantom sounds. One day a heavy object rolled back and forth across the ceiling. Then lights began to appear, seemingly without any source. They shone first on one spot in the large room, then another and another. As wind eddies caught autumn's leaves and swirled them against the windows, the youngest boys whimpered inside.

Worse was to come. A child's hand—white, almost translucent, students said—appeared against a pane of glass in an entryway window. But when Miss Perkins raced to the door, she found no one.

A week later a child saw a pale face in the same location. A young boy seemed to be resting his head against the window and peering inside the schoolroom. Once again, the teacher ran to investigate; she found no one. A face or hand continued to appear, and students greeted each showing with, "There he is now, teacher!"

News spread quickly throughout town, and soon the word *ghost* escaped people's lips. Whose ghost? Some said a thirteen-year-old boy once had been beaten savagely in the schoolroom and then thrown into the cellar. Nearby residents heard his sobbing, broke in, and carried him home, where he died a few days later. Others insisted that a small boy was once made to stand in a corner as punishment. Scared and shamed, he stood there silent all day, and the teacher forgot about him when he locked the building and left. The next morning the youngster was found dead. In both versions, the boy's family moved away shortly after their son's death, and no one remembered their name.

November grays dulled the outdoors. Inside the schoolhouse, a shriek of terror sliced the air. All eyes instantly turned to the entryway. There in the open doorway stood the full figure of a young boy. Miss Perkins jumped from her seat to pursue the apparition. He retreated to the corner of the corridor near stairs leading to the attic and stood there quietly, both hands hanging loosely alongside his brown-clad body. Under disheveled hair, his blue eyes observed the young teacher. She steadied herself against the wall, then slowly edged toward him. The figure moved up the stairs. She followed. Finally close enough to grasp him, she reached out. He vanished; she fainted. (Or perhaps—she fainted; he vanished.)

Word of the Charles Street Schoolhouse Ghost had spread far beyond city limits. Newspapers from as far away as Boston and Portland ran stories, and one night reporters even camped out at the schoolhouse in hopes of a firsthand sighting of the ghost. (It chose not to oblige.) Meanwhile, the Newburyport police began to take an interest. They invited Amos Currier and several other boys to tell them what they might know.

Quite a bit, it turned out. One lad confessed that he often had sneaked out for a drink of water and, while out of the room, pressed his hand against the glass panes. Another explained that when he was absent one day, he decided to pay a visit to the school. He had intended to climb to the attic to provide some diversionary side effects, but to his surprise, the door to the schoolroom stood open and he was seen. He backed first into a corner, he explained, and then up into the attic where Miss Perkins tried to grab him before she "fainted dead away."

Police also learned that boys had climbed into trees outside the schoolhouse, caught the sun in their mirrors, and aimed the light inside the room. In the basement, they found a joist fixed so that it could strike the floor with enough force to shake desks.

The boys were neither arrested nor charged. Town officials made repairs to the building, installed a lock on the attic entryway, and insisted that the front door be kept locked while school was in session. The ghost has rested peacefully ever since.

Cat overboard!

ℰᴑ

Jacob Brown of Newburyport began his years at sea at age fifteen, as did many of his contemporaries. Aboard the ship *Bengal* on a voyage from Wales to New York, he quickly made a name for himself.

Cats sailed on ships to control the rat population, and one day the captain's favorite fell overboard. Despite the stiff breeze, Jacob leapt into the waves to rescue her. Holding the stunned cat securely under his arm, he reached for a thrown rope and in no time stood on deck. While the cat sat against the hatch grooming herself as if nothing had happened, Jacob faced the captain.

"Why did you jump overboard?" he asked.

"To save the cat," answered Jacob. "She is too good a puss to lose."

The impressed captain shook his head. "You're bound to put it through this world if anyone can!"

His prediction proved true. In the midst of a storm, Jacob was working up on the fore topsail yard when he saw the topgallant mast break off. Seeing it coming his way, he leaped into the raging sea. Once again, the crew was able to get a rope to him and pull him to safety.

"Are you hurt?" the captain inquired.

"Not a bit, sir! How could I swim if I had been? I'm shipshape and sailor-fashion."

It should come as no surprise that Jacob Brown rose quickly through the ranks and spent most of his sailing days as a shipmaster, eventually commanding the *Agate*.

A woman rounds the world

In her pocket diary, Anne Fitch Brown records the days' events as she sails with her husband, Jacob, captain of the bark *Agate*. The sun rises and sets over the Atlantic, and the vessel crosses the ocean, bound southeast for Australia around the tip of Africa. From the day the *Agate* fills her sails outside Boston Harbor in October 1869 to the day she will drop anchor in Melbourne, Australia, one hundred days will pass. But after that, who knows how long the voyage may take? It will depend on what cargo needs to be taken to which destination.

Three of the four young Brown children accompany their parents—Jacob Frederick, Carrie, and Lillie, ages eight, five, and three, respectively. The eldest, Charlie, has stayed home in Newburyport to continue his schooling. To help with the children and the running of a household on board, Sarah, the nurse, has come as well.

The 650-ton bark built a year earlier by C. H. Currier and Company in Newburyport reflects shipbuilding skills renowned the world over. Like almost all large vessels constructed in the city, the *Agate* is a freighter. But as ships have been taking on more passengers, interior finish work has become more elegant. Cabinetmakers work inside, paneling cabins in mahogany, rosewood, and black walnut. Upholstered furniture is the norm, as are draperies and carpeting.

In this setting Anne Brown creates a home for her family. Early in January 1870, she writes of making molasses candy for the children; a few days later, she bakes mince pies. After a rainfall, caught in every available receptacle, the women wash clothes and iron them. An experienced seafaring companion to her husband, as many captain's wives are, Mrs. Brown has packed books, cards, a chess set, and fabric to keep herself occupied in any leisure time she might have.

After weeks at sea, just two hundred miles from Melbourne, the wind dies away. When it picks up, it blows head on, taxing everyone's patience. Finally, on January 13, the *Agate* anchors in Hobson's Bay off Melbourne, the first of two stops in Australia.

They stay at each port for about two weeks, in Melbourne at the Globe Hotel, then in Newcastle onboard the *Agate*. The bark undergoes minor repairs and unloads and loads cargo, picking up coal at the latter port. The family, on the other hand, is swept up in a swirl of social activities as if to offset the quiet months that lie in their wake and those on the horizon.

The American consul greets them, as is customary. They

visit with old friends and new acquaintances, enjoying teas, shopping, walks in the Botanical Gardens, picnics, and horse-back riding. Charlie is never far from Mrs. Brown's thoughts, and when the mail arrives with no letters from Newburyport, she is bitterly disappointed. Fortunately, on the day they depart, another ship brings greetings from home.

On this leg of their journey eighteen passengers sail with them. Within a day many wish they were anywhere but on board the *Agate*. The seas run high. The bark pitches violently and human stomachs match her rhythm. The weather breaks, giving them hope they may yet survive, only to turn rough again for several interminable days. And then for two days not a breath of wind ripples the surface.

Anne Brown pulls out one of her bolts of fabric, cuts out three nightgowns, and begins to sew. Over the course of the next few weeks, as the vessel sails across the Pacific, she will handstitch all three, plus a chemise, two pairs of drawers, and dresses for her girls.

A fight erupts among the men, and two find themselves in irons. Shortly, one regains his freedom after promising to behave; the other vows he will rot before he asks to be released.

In April 1870, two months after weighing anchor in Australia, the *Agate* sails into Honolulu where Captain Brown hopes to sell the coal. To Anne Brown, Hawaii "looks a perfect paradise on shore," and it doesn't disappoint her. Passengers transfer to a ship bound for San Francisco. The coal is quickly sold, and the captain begins to make arrangements for another cargo. Unlike in Australia, no old friends await his wife here, but the consul and other Americans extend a warm welcome, and port-side socializing begins again. Also to Anne's delight, they are present for the opening of the Hawaiian Parliament, which only occurs every two years, and there she sees the Queen and King Kamohama.

Soon after, they sail southwest for Baker Island (on the equator, at 176 degrees west longitude), where they'll load with guano. They've been eating their livestock from the beginning of the journey, but now three sheep die of their own accord. Two days later, the goat gives birth to two kids. In less than two weeks, they arrive at Baker Island, which Mrs. Brown describes as "a desolate looking place . . . not a sign of vegetation to be seen. And we hear the eternal screeching of the birds." The fast eight-day loading cannot be fast enough, and she's appalled by the dust from the guano, which has filtered into everything on board.

They set sail for Cape Horn, stopping only briefly at Rarotonga Island, where the captain goes ashore for a bounty of fresh fruit and vegetables. The winds favor them, but the days grow colder. The crew sets up a stove in their cabin, and the children wear coats, caps, and mittens. All hands mend a spare set of sails in preparation for the storms of the Horn.

Dreary, cold days envelop the vessel, and then the gales are upon them. The sea washes over the deck; the rigging screams in the winds. One of the crew, aloft securing a sail, falls from the main yard to the deck. Yet he's more fortunate than some. He's alive, though he has broken his arm in two places and hurt his back. Anne Brown begins a cold, which worsens into a wracking cough, keeping her cabin-bound for two weeks. They pass through a snow squall, then another monstrous gale, until on July 26 she writes, "Thank Kind Providence, we are around the Horn at last."

One week later, Anne Brown stops writing. The captain continues her diary.

> Thursday, August 4. At daylight Mrs. B. rather indisposed owing to natural causes. At 1:30 P.M. a fine girl baby made its appearance on the stage of life. Mother and child doing well.

To his duties as shipmaster, Captain Jacob Bartlett Brown now adds those of nurse. Daily, he also records critical information in his wife's diary: weather, condition of wife and daughter, what he has fed Anne. "Head winds and calm. Mrs. B. and baby doing finely. Diet gruel, toast and tea, and chicken broth." Five days after her birth, they name the baby Anne, after her mother.

Early October, four months since leaving Baker Island, the *Agate* nears Liverpool. They exchange signals with one of the ships they pass and learn that France is at war with Russia, and Napoleon is a prisoner. Then they anchor and burn a blue light requesting a pilot. Three days later, the family steps on land where letters from home and even copies of Newburyport newspapers await them. The family rests in private lodgings for a month while the bark is readied for her winter transatlantic crossing.

They sail on November 12. "Fearful gales" challenge the *Agate,* her crew, and passengers on the last crossing of the journey. Even the captain swears he will never again cross the Western Sea in winter. After one storm, "the most dreadful hurricane," Mrs. Brown goes on deck to find the sails shredded, and a mast and yard simply gone. The weather breaks, but in mid-December Captain Brown falls ill with a severe cold. As they sail through Massachusetts Bay, it begins to snow, and after fourteen months at sea they have to wait yet one more day when they reach Boston before a pilot boat can steam them safely into the harbor.

On December 20 Mrs. Brown writes, "Rejoiced are we all, I can tell you, to be so near home." And then they step back onto the soil of the United States of America.

❧

After sailing on various ships to China, Australia, and the Orient, in 1879, Charles Brown (Charlie, who had remained in Newburyport) was made captain of the same bark, *Agate.* A few years later, his bride sailed with him for their honeymoon, but their firstborn, Mary *Agate* Brown, obliged them by being born on terra firma.

Anne Bartlett Brown, born aboard the *Agate,* died on February 15, 1962, just a few months shy of her ninety-second birthday.

Wreck of the *Tennyson*

❦

"Cut away the mainmast!" screamed Captain Edward Graves over the roar of the wind. No sailor had time to obey his last command. The ship *Tennyson* settled and then began to go down by the head. A colossal wave washed away the captain and second officer William Noyes; the captain was never seen again.

Five weeks' sail from Calcutta, heading toward the Cape of Good Hope, the Currier-built ship had run afoul of the gale. As the afternoon progressed, the winds blew more ferociously. The crew followed orders to shorten and furl sails, until only the main topsail remained. They cut away the mizzenmast as directed. The lee rail dipped underwater. Then the *Tennyson* rolled heavily, and the sea burst the side of the cabin. Spars and water casks broke loose on deck. Around midnight, February 22, 1873, it was over for all but three of the twenty-four men on board.

Three survivors, William Noyes of Newburyport among them, managed to swim to a piece of the poop deck, torn loose of the ship and now floating upside-down. Day one, day two dragged by. While the tumultuous sea tossed the makeshift raft, the men fought twisting hunger. They turned their heads skyward or tried to catch rain in their palms. Periodically, they took off clothing and wrung it into their parched mouths.

After three days, the rain stopped. The men caught a seabird, but very soon thirst dominated every conscious moment. They lay curled up on their sides, trying to suck any remaining moisture from their shirts, but it was gone. Day four, day five, day six passed. Their skin grew pale, cool, and clammy, their breathing fast and shallow. Day seven passed. Day eight dawned.

William Noyes shifted restlessly on the raft. Suddenly he saw white sails on the horizon. The men could barely lift their heads. They tried to wave and then watched as the vessel sailed past them. They sank back to the boards, not moving.

The survivors of the *Tennyson* had no way of knowing that the captain of the westward-bound bark had just come on deck. He surveyed the sea, saw an odd speck in the distance, immediately brought the ship to, and headed toward the floating wreckage. Just before dark ended the eighth day, the crew of the *Warren Hastings* carefully pulled the dying men to safety.

Weeks later, Captain Edward Graves's brother received depositions from the survivors. Thus Captain William Graves—twice mayor of Newburyport and grandfather of architect William Graves Perry—learned not only that his ship had foundered in the Indian Ocean, but that he had lost his brother as well.

Chipman Silver Mines

℧

Students from Governor Dummer Academy in Newbury first discovered silver ore in town at Ox-pasture Hill. Their teacher contacted the state geologist, one Professor Hitchcock, who announced there was nothing to it, and that was that.

A generation later, in the early 1870s, Edward Rogers came across some argentiferous lead. With a neighbor, he poked around the land secretly since it wasn't his. When they thought they had found a vein, they promptly bought the acreage, formed a company, and began work. Up went a boardinghouse, blacksmith shop, and shaft houses. Down went a shaft, forty feet deep. On adjoining land, they discovered another vein. A ton of ore yielded forty pounds of silver, half an ounce of gold, and 1,200 pounds of lead, a total value of $154.

Dollar signs sparkled in people's eyes, and serious land speculation began. At one point in 1875, a farmer on Turkey Hill offered his property for $1,000 an acre. In the same year, the company, valued at $1 million, was sold to out-of-town parties and named Chipman Silver Mining Company of Newburyport.

At the height of the boom, it employed close to one hundred people, while elsewhere another two to three hundred men had work on smaller operations or as surveyors.

Clearly the time was ripe for celebration, and the city declared a half-holiday on June 2 and planned a parade. Teams of oxen pulling six tons of ore to schooners tied at the wharves were met by a procession of horses, a squad of policemen, and a brass band. Banners and flags fluttered from houses and stores along the route, and folks lining the streets cheered and clapped. To augment its long tradition of silversmithing, Newburyport now had its own native silver.

Two years later reality tarnished the promising shine. Silver extracted from the Chipman mines was found to be of low grade, but, worse yet, the precious mineral had been discovered in vast quantities out west. Locally, the quickly erected buildings stood empty, the shafts silent, deep graves filled with dreams. A decade later, the land was sold as "rocky pasture" once again.

Despite a poet's best wishes
✿

John Greenleaf Whittier, Quaker poet and abolitionist, was unable to attend the launching in 1869 of the ship *Whittier* named in his honor. He sent his regrets along with wishes that "the Merrimack give her a kindly welcome . . . [and that] she should have none but prosperous voyages."

The 1,295-ton ship was the eighty-first built by John Currier, Jr. Just shy of two hundred feet, she was owned by the three Cushing brothers: John N., William, and the Honorable Caleb (Newburyport's first mayor). She left the city under the command of Captain Swap, who had sailed the owners' other ships for twenty-one years.

On her first voyage, she took cargo from St. John, New Brunswick, to Liverpool, England. Subsequent voyages took her to cities as far away as Calcutta and Bombay. In March 1875, she departed New York, destination San Francisco, with a general cargo on board. The first two months of her trip were largely uneventful, just the occasional heavy squall and high seas flooding the deck—nothing the crew and vessel couldn't handle.

On May 18, however, as the *Whittier* sailed along the South American coast, the captain recorded something quite different in his log: "Called all hands as ship is on fire below." Large quantities of smoke rose out of the fore and aft hatches. The crew closed all hatches, hoping they could smother the fire, and the vessel immediately set course for the Rio de la Plata.

Hours later, the smoke had died down, and the men opened the fore hatch hoping to discover where the fire was burning. The air was foul, and the light in the lantern would not burn. Holding a wet sponge to his nose, the first mate made several attempts to investigate, but the fumes and lack of light drove him away. The crew closed the hatches tight once more, and everyone slept on deck that night.

At one point the following day, the smoke seeped out of every crevice on the ship. Captain Swap gave the order to lower the boats, but then the fire died down again. In light wind, the *Whittier* sailed with every square foot of available canvas, and the coast of Uruguay drew near.

On May 20, the ship took on a pilot for Montevideo. Meanwhile, the fire continued to consume the cargo below. As the smoke increased again and the planks grew hot, all hands worked ceaselessly watering the deck.

On the fourth day, signals flew from the *Whittier's* mast: "The ship is on fire!" A steam tug came alongside to tow them to port as quickly as possible. The fire broke out through the planks two feet above the waterline on the starboard side. Desperately, the crew flooded the waterway, the gutter at the edge of the deck. Water flowed through the scuppers, down the side of the hull, and subdued the flames.

The next day brought a wind so strong the tug could not tow. She left to seek help from shore and soon returned with a fire-fighting boat and men to help. The crew threw open the fore hatch, recoiling as thick smoke poured out, and the Uruguayans aimed three powerful streams of water down into the holds. By noon they had the fire under control, and two hours later it was out.

Captain Swap ventured below, fearing what he might find. He saw destroyed, charred, and water-damaged cargo, but most painful to the shipmaster's heart was the condition of his vessel. The bow of the *Whittier* had sustained the worst damage. The ship's frame and planking had burned, in some places all the way through. The lower hold, lower deck, and the area between decks would need extensive repair, but she was salvageable.

Incredibly, the *Whittier* had survived a fire burning in her hold for five days. Shipbuilders in Montevideo rebuilt her, and in March 1876, a year after originally leaving New York, she sailed into San Francisco. Four years later, though, her sailing days ended when she struck a reef off the coast of Borneo and was declared a total loss.

He's not who you think

ॐ

On February 22, 1879, Daniel Ingalls Tenney presented a statue of George Washington to the city, and it was placed on the southeastern end of Bartlet Mall (which rhymes with "shall"). The statue is one of only two in existence where the first president is not shown astride a horse. Also old postcards reveal a rather odd detail. The original name chiseled into the base was that of the donor, Daniel I. Tenney. It took decades for the Historical Society to get permission from City Hall, which owned the statue, to put George Washington's name there and relegate Tenney's name to small letters below.

The last square-rigger

Ⓢ

In 1831, John Currier, Jr., laid the keel for his first ship, the 375-ton *Brenda*. For the next half-century, he built and sold ships not only to Newburyport investors, but to men in Boston and New York, and even one to the Peruvian government. In 1883, he completed his one-hundredth and last vessel. The ship *Mary L. Cushing*, named after the wife of her principal owner, John N. Cushing, was 242 feet long, longer than the U.S.S. *Constitution*. She had a smaller displacement, however—1,710 tons, compared with the navy frigate's 2,200. With a frame of white oak, and planking and ceilings made of white pine, the *Cushing* was built to carry 2,500 tons of cargo. The first freight she carried was oil sent from Philadelphia to Japan.

Since the seaworthiness of the ship was beyond question, it was the interior, which was even more elegant than the norm, that attracted the public's attention. The forward cabin was finished in ash, and the saloon was paneled with polished bird's-eye maple and trimmed in rosewood and black walnut. Red plush upholstery covered the furniture. And the pièce de résistance was an upright piano.

While the quarters for Captain Lawrence Brown, his wife, and daughter assured their comfort, accommodations for the crew had also improved significantly over the decades since Currier's first ship. They were roomy, well-ventilated, and light.

As the *Mary L. Cushing* slid off the launching way into salt water, Currier likely knew that she was his last ship. One of the most prolific builders of wooden vessels in the country, he closed his yard shortly thereafter. It was never used as a shipyard again.

Neither Currier nor anyone else could have known that the three-masted, square-rigged *Mary L. Cushing* would be not only his last wooden ship, but also the last one built on the Merrimack and in Massachusetts.

Plum Island rescue

❦

Plum Island stretches like a narrow sandy finger for eight miles along Ipswich Bay. On a stormy day, it draws scores of people, who stand buffeted by the wind, admiring massive breakers. Some waves curl their edges into white froth a hundred yards offshore, but most crash with awesome force onto the beach.

In the days of sailing vessels, men feared this power rather than admired it. Plum Island was the site of well over a hundred shipping disasters, and a life-saving station stood at each end of the barrier beach to help rescue stranded sailors.

About noon on July 4, 1895, the *Abbie and Eva Hooper,* a three-masted schooner carrying 460 tons of coal from Philadelphia to Amesbury, sailed into Ipswich Bay and set her colors, signaling her request for a tug. By early evening, a tug began to tow her in, but the sea ran wild, breaking repeatedly over the laboring boat, and a strong easterly wind blew both vessels ever closer to the beach. Several enormous waves swamped the tug, filled her engine rooms with two feet of water, and made it impossible for the fireman to make any steam. The tug's captain had to let the schooner go in order to save his own boat from sinking. The captain of the *Abbie and Eva Hooper* had no idea he had been released until he saw the tug steaming up the river. Immediately he dropped two anchors and raised flags of distress.

Captain Noyes, who was manning the Plum Island life-saving station, was a step ahead. He had been watching both vessels, and as soon as he saw the tugboat leave, he feared the worst for the schooner. He phoned into the city to summon his crew and readied the beach cart and its equipment. Men hurried from their homes in Joppa to the station.

Perhaps the *Hooper's* anchors slowed her fate, but not for long. The seas swept her onto a sandbar close to shore, but the

First they sent the captain's eight-year-old son to safety. Then, one at a time, they climbed in, sat in the breeches, and swung down to land.

surf was so high the men could not launch a lifeboat to bring her crew to safety. Luckily, she lay within six hundred yards of land, close enough so they could prepare the lifelines instead.

In town some may have thought the sound of rockets firing was a late-night celebration of Independence Day. It wasn't. On Plum Island, the life-saving crew loaded the Lyle gun with an eighteen-pound weight to which they attached the shot line. They fired over the foundering schooner, aiming to get the weight caught in the rigging. They missed. An enormous breaker shifted the vessel, and everyone watching stopped breathing for a moment, fearing disaster. But the *Hooper* rested still once more, and finally, on the fifth try, the men onshore heard jubilant cries from the vessel's crew as they pulled the length of lightweight line until the attached heavier rope rested in their hands. This they secured to one of the highest points on the schooner, all while the wind screamed around them and waves pounded the hull.

Next the rescuers tied the breeches buoy to the line. Quickly the crew pulled the life ring with its canvas "breeches" suspended below toward themselves. First they sent the captain's eight-year-old son to safety. Then, one at a time, they climbed in, sat in the breeches, and swung down to land. The rescue was complete, except for one final crew member who stood along the rail terrified of drowning and equally terrified of bouncing through the dark over the storming sea.

One of the life-saving crew climbed into the breeches buoy and instructed his friends to pull him out to the vessel. Once aboard he told the sailor that orders were orders, grabbed him, stuffed him into the life ring, and sent him down. Shortly after midnight, the life-saver himself stepped onto firm land.

In the days that followed, hundreds came to view the *Abbie and Eva Hooper* resting serenely, bow forward on the sand, belying the dangers she and her crew had survived. Steam tugs and lighters removed part of her cargo, and eight days later at high tide a tug managed to move her off the beach and take her to Boston for repairs.

Town crier

ꙮ

At an early age, Enoch Flanders had a stroke. Permanent damage to one side left him unable to continue working as a caulker of vessels. Instead, in 1872, he took over an occupation more frequently seen in earlier times, that of town crier. For over forty years, citizens could hear him about town. Placing himself on a busy corner, he would ring his large bell and then call out his message. "Hear what I have to say! Don't forget to attend the grand ball tonight at City Hall! Tickets only fifty cents. Come one, come everybody!" City officials and merchants hired him to make announcements of all types—excursions, rallies, meetings, store bargains—keeping him busy from morning until dusk. When he died in 1914, it was said that Enoch Flanders was the second-to-last town crier in the state.

The Saltwater Gold Scam

ꙮ

Rev. Prescott F. Jernegan let it be known that he had discovered the recipe for wealth: Treat quicksilver with a secret formula and mix this solution with seawater; then pass electricity through the water and extract lots of gold along with a little silver and platinum.

It had long been known that trace amounts of precious metals could be found in the ocean, approximately one-half grain of gold per ton of seawater. However, given the proportions, no one had yet discovered how to entice the ocean to share its riches.

In February 1897, Jernegan demonstrated his new-found technique to a wealthy associate and to his friend Arthur Ryan, a successful jeweler and deacon of the First Baptist Church in Middleton, Connecticut, where Jernegan had recently served as minister. Jernegan suspended a specially designed black box with its ingredients off a wharf as the tide was coming in. In the morning, they hauled up the box and took the contents to a chemist (not chosen by Jernegan) who reported the presence of gold worth $4.50. Over the course of the year, Jernegan repeated the demonstration many times along the New England coast, intriguing scores of respected and savvy businessmen. In November a group met in Portland, Maine, and formed a corporation, the Electrolytic Marine Salts Company, with Arthur Ryan as president. Jernegan would serve as general manager, and his recently surfaced old friend, Charles Fisher, would be his assistant. Two prominent Newburyport men were among the officers of the company: Mr. W. R. Usher, treasurer, and Albert P. Sawyer, clerk and financial agent.

The factory was constructed in Lubec, Maine, a town known for exceptionally high tides. With extraordinary speed workers built a 700-foot dam and large retention basins, and below a refurbished grist mill, they hung 243 black boxes. Every week yielded over $2,000 worth of gold. Shares sold fast and nowhere faster than in Newburyport, where residents, both wealthy and of far lesser means, invested in two-thirds of the company's stock, close to $500,000 worth.

Beginning in late July 1898, startling news of the Electrolytic Marine Salts Company forced aside daily updates on the Spanish-American War. Rev. Prescott F. Jernegan had sailed to Europe, the *Newburyport Daily News* announced, "under suspicious circumstances" (an assumed name), carrying with him $338,378.40 of the company's money. He had shared his plans with no one. Mr. Sawyer, one of the directors, quickly reassured anyone who might find this news disconcerting that nothing was amiss: the money legitimately belonged to Jernegan. Besides, he noted, inventors tend to be eccentric.

The next day, papers up and down the Northeast coast announced that Jernegan's close friend, assistant general manager Charles Fisher, also was missing. The men had departed for New York together, and while Jernegan sailed away, Fisher announced that he was off to relax in the Adirondacks.

By July 30, the plant in Lubec was shut down because for the first time, the accumulators were found to contain no gold. No new company shares were being sold. Investors began to pose the question of "salting." Had gold been fraudulently introduced into the accumulators? "Impossible," the directors insisted.

After bankers in New York linked some peculiar money transactions with Jernegan, officials wired an arrest warrant to police in Le Havre, France, asking them to detain Jernegan upon arrival. Fisher was nowhere to be found, but a close friend of Jernegan and Fisher spilled the beans. On the night back in February 1897 when Arthur Ryan had sat in a shack on the wharf to witness the first demonstration, Fisher dove underwater, not to fish, but to bait. He placed gold in the black box. Fisher repeated this maneuver each time Jernegan met with investors-to-be, and although no one quite figured out how, he salted the contents of the boxes in Lubec as well.

Where Fisher had obtained such significant quantities of gold without arousing suspicion remained a mystery. Remembering his frequent trips all over the country, some wondered whether he had been buying secondhand gold jewelry to melt down.

The police in Le Havre did not arrest Jernegan because of problems with the paperwork. He traveled on to Paris and the police followed, but not very carefully, it seems. Jernegan got off the train somewhere along the way.

Back in New England, the directors of the Electrolytic

Marine Salts Company acknowledged publicly that they and all the investors had been duped. However, they also let it be known that the money Jernegan had taken was in fact legitimately his according to his contract. Jernegan could not be charged with embezzlement, and obtaining money under false pretenses was not an extraditable offense.

Meanwhile, Jernegan, son of a prominent and respected seafaring family of Edgartown on Martha's Vineyard, graduate of Brown University, and ordained minister of the Baptist Church, was having trouble with his conscience. He sent back $75,000, even though the money was technically his. Charles Fisher, on the other hand, was never heard from again.

Directors Usher and Sawyer of Newburyport returned all monies they had received. When the financial affairs of the corporation were settled, investors realized twenty cents on each dollar invested. Despite losses, many townspeople, including some shareholders, viewed the Saltwater Gold Scam with some admiration, and the paper referred to it as the "most perfect and alluring swindle."

Old elm of Newbury

☙

Richard Jaques lingered longer than he had intended at Elizabeth Knight's home. When he left his fiancée, he stepped into a moonless night. Story has it, he pulled a sapling growing next to her doorway and used it for a walking stick as he made his way down the uneven roadway. Upon reaching home, he was about to toss the young tree, but he remembered whence it came and protected its roots in some soil overnight. The next morning, he planted the elm sapling by his home on Parker Street.

Shortly thereafter, in 1713, he and Elizabeth wed. The tree flourished, and over the years it became a favorite meeting place for couples in love. Its circumference grew to over seventeen feet. It reached eighty-five feet toward the sky and spread its boughs ninety-six feet from tip to tip. In 1885, an ice storm compromised the tree's symmetry, and five years later, another gale caused further damage. Finally, in the winter of 1902, the old elm died, succumbing to age and the harshness of nature.

Twentieth Century

Pushing his wheelbarrow ahead, he traverses New England.

Colonial Jack, long distance walker

⁗

The man: Newburyport resident John A. Krohn, sometimes dressed in full Colonial costume.

The goal: To walk the 9,000-mile perimeter of the United States in 400 days (not traveling on Sundays) and return home to write about it.

The equipment: A wheelbarrow, a pyramid-shaped box mounted on a wheel, covered with business cards and flyers for which advertisers paid a dollar a piece. Inside are his necessities, plus letters people give him along the way to deliver by "leg express."

The companion: His wife, who travels separately by train and meets up with him every Sunday.

On May 30, 1908, "Colonial Jack" waves good-bye to a crowd of well-wishers in Portland, Maine, and begins his long-distance walk, which will take him to 1,209 cities and towns.

Pushing his wheelbarrow ahead, he traverses New England. Meredith, New Hampshire, he notes, "is as quiet and dead a place as I was ever in. I only saw one person laugh in the whole town, and I was informed that he did not belong there." He walks past the rolling pastures of Vermont into New York, where orchards and fields of berries stretch to the horizon. In the weeks to come, he'll pass acres of potatoes, beets, wheat, and corn. Months later, sugar, tobacco, and cotton plantations will flank his route.

He walks on roads but also frequently along railroad tracks. Some of the bridges he crosses he shares with trains to whom he "always gives the right of way." A number of these encounters are hair-raising. He finds himself in the middle of a single-track bridge and hears the locomotive approaching. Quickly he hangs the wheelbarrow by a strap over the side while he himself lies next to the guardrail and prays as the train rumbles past.

Adventures and challenges fill the weeks. In the first days, the sun burns his face, lips, and arms. Pain cramps the muscles of his legs, and blisters on his feet balloon and burst. But he walks on. At one point in his fourth week on the road, with no house in sight and his throat parched, he hops a fence, approaches a cow with a tin cup in his hand, and milks her, promptly satisfying his thirst. A few days later, a huge snapping turtle grabs and punctures the rubber tire on his wheelbarrow.

In Wisconsin he encounters a wind storm so fierce that his face and hands begin to bleed from the pelting sand. Coiled-up rattlesnakes greet him on the trail through Fort Peck Indian Reservation. Without hesitating, Jack empties his revolver and pushes on. November finds him in Idaho drenched by endless days of rain. Mrs. Krohn falls ill and returns to Newburyport for medical treatment, and her husband trudges on, his spirits sinking even lower when residents warn him that the rainy season is *coming.*

Tramps in Washington attempt a holdup, but Jack's gun convinces them to alter their plans. Oregon and California join the list of states he has passed through, and Jack enters desert country, pushing his wheelbarrow loaded with additional supplies. He fears the heat, coyotes, scorpions, and snakes, but on he goes. It will take him forty-two days to cross 1,282 miles, and he will lose seventeen pounds. It is by far the hardest part of his walk.

Engineers, alerted to Jack's journey, stop their trains to resupply him with water. At one point in Texas, he takes a recommended short cut that will trim ten miles from his journey, but he gets hopelessly lost. His water gone, he wanders around for eight hours, becoming increasingly dehydrated. He hangs a note around his neck with names of next of kin to be notified when his body is found. Then he stumbles upon old wagon tracks and follows them until he collapses. Fortunately for Jack, a prospector's camp is just up ahead. He finds our long-distance walker and, providing water, sip by cautious sip, helps him regain his health.

The prospector and the train men are among dozens of people who offer assistance. Doctors give him free medical care, and many enthusiastic innkeepers and citizens offer free room and board. In one town a sheriff arrests him as a "highway man" and sentences him to one meal in the county jail, a feast he never forgets. A few have taken advantage of him, of course, knowing that they were the only ones for miles around from whom he could buy a meal.

The journey continues through Louisiana, Mississippi, Alabama, Florida. Finally, his shadow precedes him as he turns north. And then in South Carolina, after a year on the road, he is robbed. By a hog. He leaves his wheelbarrow outside while he buys himself a meal, and when he returns it is empty, the contents scattered. The pig stands nearby, preparing to shred his raincoat.

Summer heat slows Jack, but he can now measure the distance that remains in hundreds of miles rather than thousands. In New Jersey his wife rejoins him, and their Sunday dates resume. And then, in the first week of July, he walks into Newburyport. The proprietor of the Wolfe Tavern is among the first to meet him, inviting him to stay at the hotel. Jack thanks him but declines, for up the road a little figure is running toward him, and his eight-year-old daughter leaps into his arms.

Market Square buzzes with the news of his return. The slaps on the back and shaking of hands are almost more tiring than the walking. That night his wheelbarrow rests in his in-laws' front yard, and hundreds come by to see it.

He's back on the road, his final destination Portland, Maine, where he began. As he crosses the city line, hundreds of spectators cheer. "Happy!" he writes. "Yes. That does not express it."

Jack walked for 357 days and covered 9,024 miles.

He wore out eleven pairs of shoes, and five wheels, and three tires for his wheelbarrow.

Bossy Gillis, more than a bad boy

Oɴ July 6, 1925, Andrew Joseph "Bossy" Gillis confronted Newburyport Mayor Michael Cashman at City Hall. Perhaps the summer heat had raised Bossy's inner temperature. More likely, though, resentment, which had simmered for years, finally boiled over. They argued over Gillis's property on the corner of State Street and High Street. The first punch remains in dispute, but Gillis landed several. "If you've never socked a mayor in the mush, you haven't lived," he claimed.

As a result of the altercation, Bossy Gillis would live in county jail for two months. But by fall he was back in Newburyport; in fact, he ran for city council, though he lost.

The battle over his property was far from over. Its beginning dated back to shortly after Andrew Gillis was born. His mother, Hannah, came to the city in the 1890s, a seventeen-year-old Irish immigrant with ten dollars in her pocket. She married young, gave birth to Andrew, and was abandoned by her husband. To support herself and her young son, she found employment as a domestic in the Simpson home on the corner of State Street and High Street. Determined to break out of the poverty in which so many immigrants lived, she went on to work both in a shoe factory and as pastry cook in the Garrison Inn. She skimped and saved until she and her young son could move out of the tenement into their own home on Middle Street, where she ran a grocery store. By the time Bossy was an adult, she had the means to purchase none other than the Simpson home.

Bossy promptly announced that he would raze the house where his mother once had worked as a maid and replace it with a gas station. High Street residents responded with horror. Twice the city council denied him a permit. Bossy then covered the exterior of the mansion with posters of the circus coming to town. The gables sported chamber pots, and a mock graveyard of city officials filled the grounds. After his fight with Mayor Cashman and the stint in jail, Gillis went ahead and put up a gas pump anyway. Officials promptly arrested him, fined him, and sentenced him to thirty days in jail.

This, Bossy insisted, is what killed his mother. "The folks that ran things were bound that they'd bust me," he wrote. "They didn't mind if they busted my mother at the same time. . . . When I found her dead, I made up my mind I'd make Newburyport eat out of a Gillis hand. . . . The politicians that had made life miserable for my mother would all land on the ash heap."

Gillis changed tactics. He removed the pump, and the district attorney dropped the charges. Then Bossy ran for mayor. His slogan: "A square deal for all!" A *Newburyport News* front-page editorial just prior to the election warned, "God help the city and all of us [if Gillis wins]." Hundreds of voters apparently did not concur. Andrew Joseph Gillis beat incumbent Oscar Nelson handily, 2,852 to 2,357, in the largest turnout the city had ever seen.

Gillis swept through city government, tossing out enemies and replacing them with his supporters. He ordered that no city business be done with former mayor Cashman's stables. "We'll hire no Cashman plugs except in 'dire emergencies' . . . a storm that stops everything from railroad trains to the town clock. Then wait till every other horse in Newburyport is dead from exhaustion. After that, ask me, and maybe we'll do business with Cashman." Six months after assuming the executive position, having already moved the Simpson house, he brought up the issue of rezoning so that he could run his gas station. The city council defeated the motion.

Nevertheless, the next morning, under Bossy's ax-waving

direction, the city tree department removed the old elms from the property. Shortly thereafter, he installed tanks and pumps and began selling gasoline. Arrest, conviction, appeal, and sentencing followed. Mayor Andrew Gillis of Newburyport found himself back in jail.

Gillis was no stranger to the media, who relished his plain talk and fighting spirit. Newspapers around the country covered his incarceration. Upon his release, 45,000 people packed the streets for his homecoming parade, though Newburyport itself had only 14,000 residents. In 1929, not only did Bossy get re-elected, but his candidates won city council seats. They changed the zoning law, and finally the gas station opened for business.

Andrew Gillis was far more than a scrapper with a vengeful streak, though. His mother raised him to value every hard-earned dime, and he brought this frugality with him to City Hall. As the depression tightened its grip on the country and his city, he cut back the budget. When there was no money for a lawn mower, he put a cow out to graze on the city square. When funds for fuel were depleted, he could be found in his office wearing his overcoat.

His public persona remained that of a bad-mouthed, tough kid. Those who knew him poorly or not at all came looking for that individual, and Bossy served up what they ordered. Friends and supporters—those who called him Andrew, never Bossy— knew another side. Andrew Gillis kept his good deeds quiet, sometimes anonymous. During the depression, families suffering desperate days found their coal bins filled and bags of groceries on their doorsteps. He loved kids, and prior to Thanksgiving they flocked to City Hall, where the mayor handed out food by the armful.

Newburyporters today recall Bossy Gillis as a "good man," someone "who never stole a dime," and "who would give friends the shirt off his back." Others lament that his bad-boy-mayor antics reflected poorly on the city, and some note that ultimately Bossy was his own worst enemy. All agree that Andrew Joseph Gillis was controversial.

Less than a month after Gillis first became mayor of Newburyport, he wrote a fourteen-installment autobiography published by the *Boston Herald*. In his last chapter he outlined his administration's goals. They encompassed far more than opening a gas station and destroying his enemies. "Most of all, I want Newburyport to be a place where any red-headed, two-fisted kid will be given a fair break to be somebody. No matter who their mothers and fathers are, I want kids to grow up without the tossing around that made me the roughneck I am supposed to be."

Andrew Gillis ran in twenty mayoral campaigns and won six; the last victory came in 1957. He died one day after losing the 1965 race.

Rumrunners

The story is told of a butcher shop on State Street where you could buy more than meat during Prohibition. Several men stood behind the counter, ready to assist a customer. If you approached any one of the two or three on the left, you'd get the pound of chuck you requested, but if you asked the same of the last man on the right, he would go into a back room and return with a package wrapped in white paper. It cost more than meat.

The most common refrain heard from Newburyporters versed in history is "Oh, everyone knew about it." Everyone knew the main rumrunner in town. Everyone knew the drop-off points. Not since the Embargo of 1807 had respectable Newburyport citizens so openly flouted the law. And they certainly weren't an anomaly. The Coast Guard estimates that rumrunners likely worked along every mile of the United States coast at one point or another between 1920 and 1934, the dry years.

The Merrimack River and the extensive salt marshes behind Plum Island provided rumrunners with perfect drop-off points. Fast, black boats, usually under forty feet, motored out to

European or Canadian "mother ships" anchored in international waters. They placed their orders, loaded up, and returned to shore under cover of night. Some tell of bootleggers unloading brazenly right in the center of town by Market Square. But usually, the rumrunners donned a cloak of pseudo-secrecy, picking secluded spots upriver, such as at Moseley Pines.

To keep their activities hidden, perhaps even from those who ran the show in town, smugglers chose the creeks of Plum Island Sound. Beach cottage residents report seeing lights signaling at night from sea to shore. In January 1924, authorities came upon a nameless, unregistered thirty-six-foot motorboat stranded on Plum Island with 1,500 gallons of alcohol on board. (The crew had not waited around for help to refloat their vessel.) On the same day, the Coast Guard found an additional 1,000 gallons hidden under a haystack on the island. Men made excellent money breaking a law for which they had no use. One truck run from Newburyport to Boston could net the driver $400. But Prohibition also engaged the most unlikely of lawbreakers.

At the end of a little-traveled dirt road snaking through the salt marsh in Newbury stood a lone cottage. A creek led away from the home, out toward the Parker River and Ipswich Bay beyond. An elderly lady resided within, subsisting on a tiny income. Late one night, she woke to noises downstairs and a rumble of male voices. "What's going on down there?" she called.

"Don't worry, lady," came the response. "You have nothing to fear. You just stay right upstairs, and we'll make it right with you."

The woman stayed huddled in her blankets, unable to make out their words but aware of the sound of car engines in her yard. Long after silence settled over her home, she ventured down to her kitchen. There on the table lay a hundred-dollar bill.

For years, rumrunners continued to use her home as a rendezvous, rewarding her hospitality generously each time. Who knows, perhaps she even left them muffins for a midnight snack.

Miss Mary Burns

જ

Everyone knew the patient lying in bed at Anna Jaques Hospital for her less-than-pleasant disposition. In characteristic form, she lashed out at an aide. Nurse Mary Burns walked over, leaned close to her ear, and whispered something. Neither Dr. Garnett, who was present, nor the aide heard what was said, but the patient grew instantly silent and, as the doctor reports, "behaved herself for the rest of her stay."

Mary Burns, small in stature, large in reputation, worked at the hospital for fifty-two years. When people say she lived there, they mean it literally. She had two rooms on the third floor and was on call fifty weeks a year, seven days a week, twenty-four hours a day. Even if an emergency didn't summon her, patients would report looking down from their rooms and seeing her working late into the night in the X-ray room. A fellow nurse described her as "tireless . . . always on hand for anything that needed to be done." She supervised the operating room and was, for a long time, the only X-ray technician. "She could read one better than most doctors," said Dr. Garnett. The last thing she would do each night before retiring to her rooms was to check on all the patients.

An 1899 graduate of Governor Dummer Academy, Mary Burns trained as a nurse at Boston City Hospital. She began her career at Massachusetts General Hospital, moving to Anna Jaques in 1916. In those days a nurse could not be married, and other strict rules governed her life, including a requirement to regularly attend church services. A nurse's position in the hospital hierarchy was clear: she carried out doctors' orders, period. Yet respected, skilled nurses wielded significant power. Many an older Newburyporter recalls that Miss Burns and the supervisor of nurses "ran the hospital." A picture of Mary Burns hangs outside the X-ray department, with no name affixed. She probably would have liked it that way, for she was an intensely private woman.

Born on a farm in Newbury, the eldest of nine children, she became the head of the family after her parents died, taking a keen interest in the lives of her siblings and their children. She paid for several nieces and nephews to continue their educations after high school. She liked to be consulted regarding important decisions, but no one needed to know her business.

It was by chance that her siblings discovered she was to have surgery in Boston. Her niece Kay Walsh called the nursing supervisor to learn the details, but the woman, clearly sworn to secrecy, would reveal nothing until she finally consented to pass along the surgeon's name. A couple more phone calls told the family what they needed to know, and when Mary Burns woke from her anesthesia, her niece was sitting at her bedside.

On most major holidays, Miss Burns could be found at the hospital, but she took her vacation religiously every September at salt-haying time. For two weeks she returned to the farm and her childhood, raking hay better than a man could, according to her niece. She picked beach plums on Plum Island, made huge pans of jelly, and, to her siblings' distress, also made an outrageous mess. After a fortnight as Mary or Aunt Mary, she returned to the hospital, donned her uniform, and became Miss Burns.

Mary Burns died in June 1969, one year after retiring. She was eighty-four years old. Her wishes were that mourners send no flowers but rather make a memorial donation to Anna Jaques Hospital.

The old man's bank
ℰℐ

Henry Bailey Little became president of the Institution for Savings in 1899, and that's the way it stayed for a long, long, long, long time. His style could best be described as distinctive.

Among his golden rules was, "Don't lend on anything unless you can see it out the bank window." Years later, when a reporter from the *Saturday Evening Post* approached his son, Leon, to see if the bank president would agree to an interview, Mr. Little declined. "We might get deposits from people we don't know," he shuddered.

Careful investment and management paid off, though. During the early years of the depression, over two thousand banks failed, in large part because depositors panicked and there was a run on banks. In March 1933, to avoid further calamities, President Roosevelt closed every bank in the nation. Gradually, as state bank examiners deemed a bank solvent, it would resume business. The Institute for Savings in Newburyport was the second bank in the United States permitted to reopen.

When now-retired bank president John Pramberg, Jr., began his career at the Institute as a teller in 1955, the bank operated "like something out of Dickens." Seven elderly gentlemen filled all the positions, while one woman answered the phone and did their typing. All posting was done by hand, using steel-point pens dipped in imported Stevens ink—no other. Except for replacing gas lights with electricity, the bank had not been remodeled since 1902. Yet H. B. Little was not someone stuck in the past. He quickly embraced some modern conveniences, such as the telephone, oil furnace, and electric refrigerator, but he was selective, choosing never to own either a radio or a television.

Mr. Little continued to arrive at work in his black car decades after most men his age had retired. Joseph, his chauffeur, opened the car door, and out stepped H. B., dressed meticulously in blue, a stiffly starched white wing collar pressing up into his chin. In the warm months, he wore his straw hat, so old it had numerous holes in its brim. "There's absolutely no reason for me to buy a new hat at my age," he claimed, as frugal in his personal life as he was in the management of the bank's finances.

But this story concerns not a day when Mr. Little arrived at his bank, but rather a day when he traveled away from it. A decision was made that the bank's bonds should thenceforth be kept in Boston. Accordingly, Mr. Little, then in his early eighties, together with the bank's treasurer, Mr. Balch (a much younger gentleman in his sixties), decided to deliver the papers personally. The bank president carefully placed $7 million of negotiable bonds in a straw suitcase and summoned Joseph.

The chauffeur brought them to the depot, where the two men boarded the train. In Boston, a cab took them on the final leg of their journey. Once inside the doors of the First National Bank of Boston, Messrs. Little and Balch were courteously welcomed by an official flanked by security guards. The Bostonian seemed somewhat distracted, though. "Where are your security guards?" he asked.

"No guard," Mr. Little answered.

"Ah, you came in an armored truck?"

Mr. Little scoffed at such a suggestion. "No one is going to bother two old men," he said.

After working at the bank for fifty-four years, Mr. Little retired at age 102, the oldest bank president in the country. He died four years later, in 1957. While subsequent bank presidents have greatly expanded Mr. Little's customer base, many in town still refer to the Italianate brownstone building on State Street as "the old man's bank."

A life of design

Aram Kalashian sat on his front steps, as usual, sketch pad on his knees. And George Parker, head of the design department at Towle Silver Manufacturing Company, walked down Broad Street, as usual, to work. But this time Mr. Parker stopped, then approached the teenager he had noticed so many times and asked to look at his drawings.

He inquired when the young man would be graduating and

then suggested that Aram come see him in a year. "I'd like to have you working for Towle, and I'll see that we educate you," he said. And so it came to be. With Towle paying his expenses, the young artist took classes at the Rhode Island School of Design. He became one of the company's top designers. Only one Towle pattern is patented in an employee's name, the 1940 "Old Mirror" design by Aram Kalashian. Mr. Kalashian died in 1965, having worked at Towle his whole life, just a short walk away at the end of his street.

The hunt for German subs

Throughout most of history, vessels sailed the oceans, fishing their depths or transporting goods and people between nations and continents. As the twentieth century progressed, these craft came to be used more for pleasure than for commerce. During the Second World War, however, a number of large sailing vessels provided a critical service that matched neither of these roles.

In February 1942, Bob Henneberry of Newburyport sailed out of New York Harbor with twenty-five other navy servicemen aboard the S.S. *Vega*. Like the ten or so other ships sailing out of New York, the *Vega* was originally privately owned and had just recently been deeded to the United States Navy. The ships' mission: To find German submarines.

Hundreds of enemy subs lay in wait, twenty to thirty miles offshore, in shipping lanes all along the East Coast. Their job was to destroy American supply ships heading for beleaguered Britain. During the day, the submarines hid deep, but at night, usually between midnight and 4:00 A.M., they had to come to the surface to recharge their batteries, using diesel engines whose noise could be heard at some distance.

The sailing vessels, on the other hand, searched silently. When they heard and identified a German submarine, they radioed its position to shore, then planes flew out to bomb the intruder. The sailing ships would turn tail as quickly as possible, for any submarine's firepower was monumental by comparison to theirs. The *Vega's* crew, for example, was as good as unarmed; they carried a few rifles and side arms.

One day, shrouded by fog, the *Vega* sailed toward the coast to resupply herself with fresh water. With visibility limited to a quarter of a mile, she proceeded cautiously. The bow lookout signaled; he had heard voices ahead. The crew couldn't make out the language, nor could they see an outline of the vessel. Then to their horror the shape of a sub became visible. All ears strained until several sailors heard comforting swear words that only an American seaman could utter. The submarine was their own.

For six months, Bob Henneberry sailed the Atlantic in the predawn hours, watching and listening—hoping, no doubt, that should he be close enough to hear a voice, it would speak English.

Wolfe Tavern no more

☙

One hundred years after illustrious guests such as Oliver Wendell Holmes, Franklin Pierce, Ralph Waldo Emerson, Horace Greeley, and John Quincy Adams stayed in its rooms, the Wolfe Tavern on the corner of State and Harris Streets succumbed to demolition.

The old tavern not only served as a link with the original Wolfe Tavern, which had stood on the corner of Threadneedle Alley until it burned in the Great Fire, but had historic value of its own. In 1813 Benjamin Hale made alterations, built additions, and converted the John Peabody house of 1807 into a hotel. Since it served as a stop on the stagecoach route, business flourished.

In the same year that the hotel register listed names of

famous personages, the events in one room of the tavern offered a glimpse into lives seldom noted in history books. In mid-December 1853, hotel employees found two women dead in their bed. In a foreword to a summary of the inquest, the editor of the *Newburyport Daily Herald* wrote of them as "lost and ruined girls . . . possessed of more than ordinary beauty . . . comparative novices in vice." Testimony revealed that one of the women had a child boarding elsewhere in the city, while the other had recently sought an abortion in Boston. Both women were despondent, acquaintances said. Their deaths were ruled a double suicide as a result of drinking large quantities of alcohol stronger than proof spirit after not having eaten for the past twelve hours.

Around the same time, the tavern underwent further expansion. The tragedy appeared not to affect business, though ownership changed rather frequently. Few proprietors will be as well remembered as the final one, Robert Weltshe, who also owned the Garrison Inn. By the middle of the twentieth century, the Wolfe Tavern was struggling. Newburyport, in general, was facing economic hardship, and construction of the Route 1 bypass diverted traffic from the center of town. Now travelers heading north no longer passed the tavern on State Street. Mr. Weltshe got into a dispute with City Hall over a liquor license, and when the city rejected the application, he threatened to tear the tavern down. No one believed he would. He did.

First, in September 1953, he advertised "The Outstanding Auction of the Year"—the contents of the 150-year-old hotel. Then, in early October, dismantling began. The event drew little public interest; the newspaper didn't even note it.

Four years later, Rosamond Snow, president of the Historical Society of Old Newbury, was quoted by the *Newburyport Daily News* as saying she "hoped the razing of the Wolfe Tavern would serve as a lesson, so that other old buildings would not be lost to Newburyport." It may have done just that, as the events of the 1960s would bear out.

Long-time residents of the city remember the tavern well. Men tell of the old stagecoach parked in the driveway, and all who speak of the old tavern shake their heads with regret.

Margaret Cushing, centenarian

When Margaret Cushing celebrated her one-hundredth birthday, President Eisenhower sent his congratulations, as did the governor of Massachusetts. She stood in the doorway of her home on High Street, her carriage as erect as ever, while city bells pealed one hundred times by order of Mayor Graf.

In her hundredth year, she continued to serve on two boards and held the meetings in her parlor, greeting everyone graciously and assigning seats. Everyone had his or her place, and she knew hers.

Margaret Cushing was tremendously proud of her heritage. Her grandfather, John Newmarch Cushing, had risen to prominence along with Newburyport. The son of a Salisbury farmer, he went to sea as an eight-year-old cabin boy. By age twenty he was shipmaster, and at age thirty he was part-owner of a ship. He bought the Federalist mansion on High Street in 1818. Margaret's father and his brother, Lawrence, were among the city's most successful shipowners, prospering when shipbuilding was at its peak. And her Uncle Caleb chose a career of public service. He was elected to the state legislature and the U.S. Congress and served as mayor of Newburyport. He was appointed commissioner to China, associate justice of the Supreme Judicial Court, Attorney General of the United States during President Franklin Pierce's administration, and minister to Spain.

Miss Cushing preserved her home as though to capture their lives. She altered nothing. Wallpaper, window treatments, floors, and carpeting remained the same throughout her adult life. She would not allow electricity to be installed, so her servants cooked on a wood stove in the basement kitchen until the day Margaret died. She had no indoor plumbing. Finally, when the Board of Health ordered it, she indignantly agreed to install a toilet and small washbowl in a basement closet. She never used them, however. She could see no reason whatsoever for changing her habit of using the chamber pot in her bedroom.

Baths she took every Saturday at her niece's home two doors down. She could be seen walking down High Street, dressed in black as always, carrying all she needed for her toilette in a small black bag.

One day, on her way for her weekly bath, she met the Unitarian minister. She was very fond of Reverend Haywood and he of her, and the two friends put down their bags while they stood on the corner chatting. A while later they parted. When the reverend reached his study, he opened his bag to discover a towel, soap, toothbrush, and other toiletries. As the tub filled with water, Miss Cushing, in turn, found that she had with her the draft of the minister's sermon. They would laugh over the switch for years to come.

In Margaret's last decade, her family decided that she needed a live-in companion; however, the woman they had selected refused to move in unless a phone was installed for use in an emergency. Miss Cushing considered a telephone an unthinkable intrusion on her privacy, but she had little choice in the matter. She hated the contraption and only answered it if no one else was home. She held it as far away as her arm allowed and yelled, "Call back. Call back!" before quickly hanging up.

Though Margaret Cushing held modern conveniences in disdain, she thirsted for knowledge and was an avid reader, consuming books on a wide range of subjects, including works in French. Neighbors reported seeing the gas lights burning in her bedroom deep into the night. Her formal education ended with high school, but she traveled on her father's ships a number of times, and during her Uncle Caleb's years as minister to Spain, she acted as his hostess. She wrote many papers, though only a few remain, since she destroyed most of them when she was in her nineties. Miss Cushing attended lectures, concerts, and plays, often arriving just a little late and then walking down the aisle to her front-row seat. A member of the Episcopalian Church from birth, she nevertheless let it be known that had she had her own way, she would have been a Catholic.

The last seems a contradiction, for Margaret Cushing was certainly used to being in charge of her life. And yet, just as the integrity of her house was not to be tampered with, neither were the traditions of her upbringing. She was raised an Episcopalian and Episcopalian she would remain.

Margaret Cushing died a few months after her centennial birthday. Her home is now the Cushing House Museum owned by the Historical Society of Old Newbury.

Yankee Homecoming
☙

Waterfront concerts, sidewalk bazaars, dancing, and art exhibits draw thousands to the city the first week of August each year for Yankee Homecoming. Though Newburyport began the celebrations in 1958, along with dozens of other cities across New England, it has continued the festivities long after other cities have stopped. For years, a historical reenactment highlighted the week's events. Newburyport citizens portrayed George Washington's arrival in town, explorer Adolphus Greely's return from the Arctic, or the homecoming of Newburyport's Civil War soldiers. The ten-mile road race now includes thousands of runners rather than just a few dozen. Yankee Homecoming also features a firemen's muster, a kids' day at the park, and an antique auto parade. The week culminates with a parade on Sunday. Residents set up chairs and awnings along High Street the night before, staking out their territory. Some "reserve" areas by tying ropes between trees. This is an event for which one needs front-row seats!

"Mrs. Nobody"

❧

Louise Morse stands at the lectern, her hands relaxed. She has just told her audience about the time she drove to Swampscott to give a ride to a man with whom she was to attend a meeting. She knew his street. She remembered his house. But she absolutely could not recall his name. "You can imagine how relieved I was to see the brass plate with his name right above the knocker." She pauses for a beat. "It said M-O-R-S-E. Morse." And she smiles as the room bursts into laughter, men and women recalling a time when they, too, had forgotten something as simple as someone's name identical to their own.

"Who am I?" Louise Morse of Newbury used to ask. "I'm just a nobody." And so she titled her talks "Mrs. Nobody goes somewhere." At her own expense, Mrs. Morse traveled to eighty-five countries where CARE, the international relief and development agency, had programs. Upon returning to the States, she gave over two thousand talks about her trips to educational, church, and civic groups all over New England, donating her fees to CARE and spreading the word.

Gathering her listeners' attention once more, she shifts to the more serious side of her speech, a story about one of her first trips, a stop in Hong Kong. "I never anticipated what I saw for housing," she says, describing dugouts in the sides of hills and shelters built from cardboard. Just three blocks from her hotel, she stopped to take pictures of some children and then reached into her pocketbook to hand out a few coins. Swarms of little ones came from she knew not where, clawing at her hand so desperately, they scratched it till it bled.

A few hours later, she worked alongside a CARE employee

handing out food packages to one thousand refugees. At first she was stunned by the thankful expressions on people's faces, but soon she wanted simply to leave. "It was so hard to take. I felt sick doing this," she confesses to her audience. "Never in my life have I as a person had to receive gratitude, endless and endless, for just handing out a little box of somebody else's donation of food. . . . I knew the casual dollar we give without denying ourselves anything. We as a people are not worthy of being seen on such a level of goodness."

Louise Morse claimed she merely had "a little extra dash of the gift of gab." Her stories lightened lives with humor, and her tales and those told of her reveal a heart that was extra large. For this is a woman who traveled to the tropics dressed in multiple layers of clothing so that she could fill her luggage to capacity with goods for those in need.

When she arrived at her destination, she would immerse herself in CARE's activities and the people with whom the organization worked. Ralph Devone, assistant country director in Colombia in the 1960s, remembers her visiting projects in the fields, helping in mother-child programs, observing in schools, and connecting with the people, language barriers notwithstanding. Louise Morse was not someone who watched from a distance; she dove into local traditions with enthusiasm.

The night before she was to leave Colombia, the CARE staff took her out to dinner in Bogotá. One local custom during any celebration calls for a leather-covered bag of wine, a *bota,* to be passed around the table at intervals. Everyone holds the bag at arm's length and directs a stream of wine into his or her mouth, a feat that increases in difficulty as the evening wears on. "She had terrific aim," Ralph recalls, "but we couldn't figure out what she did with the wine because she remained far too sober." Thirty-five years after her visit, he laughs again as he tells the anecdote. "We always wondered if she found a way not to swallow it."

CARE estimates that through her talks, Louise Morse raised

over $1 million to fund projects around the world: water wells in India, tools in Greece, sewing machines in the Philippines, a schoolhouse in Guatemala. Mrs. Morse died in the summer of 1987; she was eighty-two years old. It took a very special somebody to be Mrs. Nobody.

Hold the wrecking ball!

Picture the brick buildings along Inn Street, along State Street, in Market Square empty and boarded up—not all, but many of them. In the hollow spaces within, the homeless seek shelter, many with flasks buried in their pockets. In the 1950s, the heart of the city, rebuilt after the Fire of 1811, was barely beating. According to former Mayor Byron Matthews, Newburyport was in a "dire economic position." Others recall a city and people in need of total revitalization.

Cities and towns across the country had long since recovered from the depression of the 1930s, but in Newburyport, another devastating fire in May 1934 had deepened the depression years. It reduced to ashes two shoe factories and multiple stores and homes, and it left five hundred additional people without work. The factories were never rebuilt. New jobs never came. For the next two decades, the city limped along. Then, in the late 1950s, CBS-Hytron, maker of television picture tubes, closed, leaving almost three thousand unemployed. Virtually no industry remained in the city.

In 1960 Mayor Albert H. Zabriskie and the city council created the five-member Newburyport Redevelopment Authority (NRA) with a directive to clean up the shabby central business district. No one foresaw that Newburyport would ultimately redefine the entire concept of urban renewal. The NRA studied the options carefully, and word began to spread that they were leaning toward demolishing the downtown area. Most peo-

Word began to spread that they were leaning toward demolishing the downtown area. Most people paid no attention. It was a mess, they said; tear it down.

ple paid no attention. It was a mess, they said; tear it down. Members of the Historical Society of Old Newbury, knowledgeable of the city's history, were appalled.

Their efforts to prevent the leveling of dozens of 150-year-old buildings began gently in 1963 with a slide presentation given by Mr. and Mrs. Edmund Burke during a reception for town officials. The slides highlighted the many noteworthy architectural features of historic Newburyport structures. A few months later, Abbott Cummings, Professor of American and New England Studies at Boston University, declared that Newburyport had the best-preserved nineteenth-century commercial district on the Atlantic seaboard, if not in the entire nation.

Members of the NRA, however, considered the dilapidated buildings an eyesore. Concerning their "supposed historical value," the director wrote that they "even detract from the value of the land on which they stand." The NRA remained steadfast in its pursuit of federal money for urban renewal. The public remained apathetic to the exchanges in the newspaper, deaf to discussions among the concerned. Then, in the summer of 1964, the NRA proudly displayed a model of their plan in a store window on State Street. It showed that all the brick buildings were to be demolished and replaced with a black-topped parking lot surrounded by a brand-new shopping center. Lovers of historic structures gasped.

The Burkes held a meeting in their home. It was clear to all involved that an organized effort was essential if the bulldozing of the old downtown was to be prevented. They formed a Committee on Renewal and Restoration under the aegis of the Historical Society, with Newburyport resident Dr. Robert Wilkins as chairman. The prestigious cardiologist would continue to play a key role in the city's renewal for years to come. The newly created committee agreed with the NRA on one thing: they too wanted to transform the depressed downtown into an economically viable commercial district. Their goal, however, was to do this while preserving the city's historic architectural integrity.

The NRA's plan for demolition and a new shopping center lay on a desk in Washington, D.C., awaiting approval for funding. Meanwhile the committee sought expert advice from William Graves Perry, architect of Colonial Williamsburg and a descendant of Newburyport sea captains. They needed to document quickly that historic restoration would work as well as the NRA's plan. Early in 1965, they presented Mr. Perry's model for preserving the facades of the buildings, and this galvanized public interest and support.

The Department of Housing and Urban Development (HUD) had just been created. The NRA had grave concerns that if they began amending their plan, they would lose their chance of getting any federal aid. But developers began to express interest, and in response federal officials were supportive. It looked as though the historical society's vision would preserve what could never have been replaced.

Years of work lay ahead. City officials voted to take twenty acres of the commercial district by eminent domain. They put up $250,000 as the city's share of redevelopment costs. In 1968, newly-elected Mayor Byron Matthews traveled to the nation's capital, restoration plans in hand, experts at his side. HUD had never funded a restoration project, but they agreed to let Newburyport try its plan on a limited scale, just on Inn Street. Federal officials loved the results, and the city went on to create history. Close to $12 million flowed in. The city bought new sidewalks, put up streetlights that are replicas of those that lit the streets a century earlier, and, most important, preserved historic buildings.

With restoration fully launched, city officials shifted their attention to attracting small companies. Never again would Newburyport be dependent on a few major industries; today the

Lord Timothy Dexter Industrial Green is home to scores of businesses.

HUD urban restoration projects followed in Baltimore, Boston, Salem, and Portsmouth, New Hampshire. Images of Newburyport's downtown, weary with age and depression, remain only in photographs and memories. Today, shops and restaurants bustle with activity. In the summer flower boxes overflow with color and life, while in the winter white lights frame the windows. It is hard to imagine now that anyone ever considered doing anything other than restoring the buildings.

Waterside addresses

Newburyporters do not live in Newburyport. They live "down-along," "up-along," or "out back" (also referred to as "over back"). State Street divides down-along and up-along. With perfect logic, down-along lies down river, the south (sort of) end of town. Down-along also includes Joppa (pronounced Joppy), where clammers and fishermen formerly lived. It stretches from Plum Island to about Federal Street. Folks who live in down-along are down-alongers. Up-alongers, therefore, reside west of State Street, upriver. Not many live "out back" or "over back" because that's primarily the industrial park, common land of long ago. And if someone doesn't live in Newburyport proper, she or he may be from "over the river" (Salisbury) or Old Town (Newbury).

The Custom House, again

❦

For over a decade in the middle of the twentieth century, the Custom House stood as a sorry symbol of Newburyport's sagging spirit. The granite structure built in 1835 by Robert Mills, designer of the Washington Monument, was owned by a junk dealer. Old motors, rolls of wire and cable, and piles of metal reached from the marble and terra cotta floors up to the vaulted ceilings. A walk up the cantilevered granite staircase led to more debris. Along the river in back, men dismantled two navy submarines and added any parts of value to the junk inside.

After the city's years as a thriving port had come to an end, the Custom House had been sold into private hands. One owner stored hay inside. At another time, the building augmented the local shoe industry by serving as a heel factory, but it was the building's use as a receptacle for junk that ultimately led to its being returned to the public.

In the early 1960s, a small group of Newburyport residents, proud of their city's past, tried to find ways to get the junk dealer out. They asked National Historic Register officials for help, but while they agreed that the building had historic value, they had no authority to do anything. Instead, Newburyport's urban renewal plan rescued the Custom House. The lines drawn for the area to be taken by eminent domain traveled down Water Street, encompassed the historic building, and came back up the street to connect with the twenty-acre rectangular district to be restored.

After the junk dealer received eviction papers, several townspeople (Edmund Burke, Rupert Nock, George Cashman, and Pete Morse among them) recognized a perfect opportunity to establish a museum in the old Custom House. They resurrected the Marine Society, which had declined with the city's shipping industry, and began raising funds to restore the building, especially its damaged interior. In June 1975 the Custom House Maritime Museum opened its doors, presenting the city's shipbuilding and seafaring history to the public.

Tunnels under town

The demolition of the house on Charter Street in 1978 was almost finished as Chip Davis maneuvered his bulldozer along the cellar wall. Instantly, he cut the engine. There behind the wall he had just taken down stood a steel door. He and his son pried it open with bars. A brick archway faced them and another door, this one wooden. They pulled it open and stepped inside a brick tunnel about six feet wide and almost that high.

Narrow English bricks, the kind that used to come over in ships as ballast, lined the walls and arched ceiling above. Davis and his son scraped underfoot and found that the floor was brick, too. A few steps from the entrance, a side tunnel branched off, heading behind them. It was the first of four they would find, less high than the central tunnel but equally wide. Each was blocked off part way down by a thick brick wall.

Father and son, with flashlights in hand, proceeded slowly down the main tunnel only to come to another blockade. This one was only one brick layer thick, and they tore part of it away so that they could go on. The tunnel now ran steeply downhill parallel to State Street. The air hung heavy and damp around them, and occasionally a large rat scurried past. They walked on for about 250 feet more, down four steps, past a three-foot-wide landing on the side, until a brick wall stopped them for the last time.

They searched carefully as they made their way back and found several artifacts, including two branding irons, one with the word *Newburyport,* the other with the initials *FEP,* presumably used to stamp barrels of rum as if they had legitimately

Story has it that tunnels ran under Federal Street, State Street, and Green Street, all leading to the waterfront.

passed through customs, which, of course, they hadn't. And that—smuggling—was the purpose of the tunnels, initially probably to avoid taxes, later to bypass an unpopular embargo, and then, quite possibly, prior to the Civil War to help runaway slaves reach ships that would sail them to Canada and freedom.

Story has it that tunnels ran under Federal Street, State Street, and Green Street, all leading to the waterfront. Chip Davis's discovery confirms the existence of one close to State Street. When working on another project, this time on Water Street, his bulldozer literally fell into a large brick chamber underground, with benches lining the perimeter and chains hanging from the wall. It lay in line with the tunnel he had found earlier. When the city replaced the sewer and water lines in the 1970s, workmen came upon several places that appeared to be caved-in tunnels. Residents have found entrances leading about twenty feet underground near the tannery and at the cemetery behind the mall. Another bricked-up entrance exists outside a home on Federal Street.

Stories of the Newburyport tunnels lie buried deep in its history and continue to circulate around the city just as remnants of the passages lie beneath the ground. The answers to who built them, how long people used them, and why they blocked them remain sealed as tightly as the tunnels themselves.

The legacy of Nicholas Arakelian

ႽჂ

To a twelve-year-old newspaper boy who worked for him, Nicholas Arakelian was a formidable individual. Antique dealer Chris Snow remembers him as tall, burly, stern, and unsmiling. To most of the world, Mr. Arakelian presented this somewhat grouchy exterior. He didn't mix easily, so it was hard to get to know him.

Four-year-old Nic and his parents came to the United States in 1894 after fleeing Turkish persecution in Armenia. In their first year, the family moved from New York to Fall River to Malden before finding a permanent home among the small Armenian community in Newburyport. Nic's father worked in one of the shoe factories, the family grew, and Nic attended school. But when he was in the eighth grade, his father was badly injured and couldn't work. The Arakelian family couldn't even afford to buy Nic the requisite white shirt for graduation from the Kelley School. Classmates raised the money, and Nic attended the ceremony which ended his formal education. He began working at Fowle's News Store on State Street.

The serious, hard-working young man so impressed Mrs. Fowle that after a few years, the widow gave him part-ownership of the store. In 1913, the federal government imposed the first income tax, and Nic Arakelian realized he needed a bookkeeper. He hired young Mary Alice Callahan, the woman who would become the love of his life.

In keeping with the times, both the Arakelian and Callahan families, as well as the Armenian and Irish Catholic communities, opposed their marriage. Nic and Mary Alice worked side by side for five, ten, fifteen, twenty years. Meanwhile, Nic acquired full ownership of Fowle's. Finally, in 1933, the couple had waited long enough. Story has it they drove to New York and found a priest to marry them.

Fowle's not only carried one of the biggest assortments of magazines north of Boston (and still does), it has always had a food counter and a soda fountain. For years, it was the favorite morning gathering spot for businessmen. Nic Arakelian also distributed papers and magazines to other stores. He managed his business frugally, invested well, and gradually amassed significant savings. The Arakelians moved to Newbury, where they built a new home on the old footing of Mary Alice's family homestead. The couple traveled extensively, taking several cruises. In 1957 Mr. Arakelian, confident his finances would provide well for

Mary Alice after his death, sold Fowle's. He never went into the store again.

Eight years later Mary Alice Arakelian died of a heart attack, leaving her husband a devastated man. Upstairs in her bedroom her nightgown, slippers, brush—everything—remained untouched. Nic Arakelian refused to part with the last car he and Mary Alice had owned together. Though he continued to meet with friends for lunch, he seemed to be watching the months fold themselves into years. Friends say that he simply never got over losing her.

Behind his reserve, Nic Arakelian was a quietly generous man. From small gestures, such as sending a free copy of the Sunday *New York Times* each week to an elderly widow, to large donations to Armenian fund-raisers, he could be counted on to contribute. His final gift was to take the money he had so carefully set aside for his wife's well-being and, with the help of his close friend John Pramberg and his accountant, create a charitable foundation in her memory.

In 1980 when Nicholas Arakelian died, the Mary Alice Arakelian Foundation, valued at $3 million, became active. By the end of the century, the foundation had grown to over $8 million. In the first two decades of its existence, it has given money to churches, education and health programs, homeless shelters, and National Public Television and Radio. Its largest donations have gone toward the restoration of the Firehouse Theatre in Market Square and the expansion of the Newburyport Public Library. Without his toughness, Nic Arakelian may not have had the means to exercise his kindness. His legacy lies in his ability to transform hardship and heartache into opportunity, if not for himself, then for others.

Transforming the firehouse

Looking at the Firehouse Center on Market Square, it may be hard to see how this building housed the Newburyport Fire Department for over one hundred years. But place an early twentieth-century photograph of the firehouse alongside one of the restored structure, and the ingenious way in which the architects incorporated the building's past life into its new one becomes clearly visible.

Four large doors through which horse-drawn fire wagons once passed are now the windows to the first-floor restaurant. Patrons enter both restaurant and the arts center through a fifth door, formerly the entrance to the police station, which also shared this space. Within the brick hose tower, where fire hoses once hung drying, stairs spiral up to the lobby and gallery, which overlook the waterfront park and the Merrimack River. The rest of the second floor is home to the Arakelian Theatre, the jewel within the arts center.

Role shifts are nothing new to this old brick building. It began its career as a one-story market house in 1822 with butchers' stalls filling its space. A year later, a second story was added, and here the Newburyport Chair Company made cane-bottom chairs for several years. Public meetings were later held here, and in the 1840s the Lyceum Association used the hall for weekly lectures. Locally prominent speakers as well as lecturers from out of town drew such large audiences that tickets had to be sold by lottery. Finally, in 1864, the public building settled into an extended run as a fire station.

When the fire department moved to its new headquarters in 1979, the building stood vacant for a while. Local businessmen saw it as the perfect location for a civic center and began a campaign to transform the old firehouse into a center for the arts that would encourage artists within the community while bringing more art from outside the city. A newly created Society for the

Development of the Arts and Humanities convinced the city not to convert the building into apartments and retail space. Then it launched an extraordinary fund-raising drive that in three years raised $760,000 from individuals and local businesses. The largest single gift of $200,000 came from the Arakelian Foundation. The Commonwealth of Massachusetts augmented the society's efforts with a grant of $1.8 million. In August 1991, the Firehouse Center opened for its premier season.

In less than a decade the Arakelian Theatre has welcomed audiences to over 2,500 performances of theatre, music, dance, and children's productions. Newburyport citizens' efforts on behalf of their arts center come not only in the form of continued financial support, but also from over 250 volunteers who take care of most of the day-to-day operations, guaranteeing that the shows will go on.

Final resting places

In the twenty-five years Lilian Kelleher worked for Helen C. Moseley as companion and nurse, she formed a close relationship with her employer. Older by a few years than Miss Moseley, she expected to die first and so approached a local funeral director to let her wishes be known. She asked Todd Woodworth to arrange that her burial be at the Sawyer Hill Burying Ground opposite the Moseley estate.

"I want to be there," she told him, "because Helen always goes by, downtown and back, two or three times a day. I want to be there so she can wave to me as she drives by." Sadly, only a part of Mrs. Kelleher's wishes could be fulfilled.

Miss Moseley died in December 1974 and lies buried with several generations of the Moseley family at Oak Hill Cemetery. Mrs. Kelleher passed away twelve years later at eighty-nine. She rests in a plot at Sawyer Hill marked on each corner by small

The sun sends dappled light through tall pines and oaks onto the azaleas.

granite squares etched with the letter *K.* Helen Moseley never waves to her, but the sun sends dappled light through tall pines and oaks onto the azaleas that blossom over her grave.

Tuesday Night Club

A group of young men in the city grew tired of waiting to be admitted to the Fortnightly Club, so in 1911 they formed their own organization, the Tuesday Night Club, and for decades since, eighteen gentlemen have met every other week except during the summer. Each member entertains the group once a year at his home and at another time writes and presents a paper. Cocktail hour begins at 7:45, followed by dinner, and then it's the essayist's turn. To conclude the evening, the host calls upon the other members to comment on the essay. In past years, writers have read biographies of famous persons, poetry, a personal essay chronicling a member's escape from war-torn Germany, a fictional mystery story, and a paper on the Isles of Shoals. Only essays on religion or politics are frowned upon. And therein may lie the secret of the club's meeting uninterruptedly for almost a century.

Lord Timothy's cupola

One August day in 1988, a wisp of smoke escaped the upper eaves of the house where Lord Timothy Dexter once lived. Owner Bill Quill saw it, and the fire department responded speedily. Painters had been blistering off paint with torches, and sparks fanned by the breeze found an easy prey in the two-century-old structure. By the time daylight gave way to darkness,

Painters had been blistering off paint with torches, and sparks fanned by the breeze found an easy prey in the two-century-old structure.

everything from the second-floor ceiling up, including the cupola, was badly burned and much of the rest of the interior water-damaged beyond repair. Only the shell of the mansion stood intact.

State fire officials, worried that the structure would collapse, suggested tearing the house down. The owner called in an expert in salvage and demolition, and together they decided to try to save Timothy Dexter's mansion, first by removing weight. Working from the roof down, a crew of nine removed the damaged materials by hand as cables held the exterior walls together.

While the owner sketched architectural features, took note of dimensions, and worried about the astronomical cost of rebuilding, a group of friends decided to rally community support by establishing a fund to help restore Lord Timothy's famous cupola. Artist Christopher Gurshin gingerly made his way about the home, collecting slates from the roof, pieces of original beams, nails, wood carvings, anything that captured his imagination. These he transformed into ingenious artifacts—a part of history for someone's home—to be sold at a fund-raising auction. Others donated additional memorabilia, and two months later people gathered on the side lawn for the bidding.

The auctioneer, dressed as Lord Timothy Dexter, raised over $8,000, but more critically, the gesture lifted spirits as well. Ultimately, repairs to the mansion, which took a year, came in below budget, and Bill Quill donated the money from the auction to the Firehouse Theatre. Carpenters reconstructed the cupola in sections in the dining room, using old photographs and drawings. They carried its eight parts up to the roof and bolted them into place. Once again the cupola graces the roof of the fully restored mansion at 201 High Street.

Each member part of a greater whole

❧

"The only thing better than sitting in the audience listening to the Newburyport Choral Society is to be a part of it," said the woman, her skin still tingling after the performance. A nurse by profession, she had never sung with a group before. But in the choral society, voice placement tests take the place of auditions, and no one has ever been turned away. The nurse joined as a second alto. "Hard work and an openness to learning are the prerequisites," explains the vice-president of the society, "not performance-quality voices," although they have those, as well.

Since 1987, under the talented direction of Boston University professor Gerald Weale, the choral society has aimed high, tackling music such as Bach's Mass in B-minor and Mozart's and Verdi's Requiems. Members learn about composers, basics of theory and timing, and expression. Above all, they are drawn by the opportunity to work on the best of choral music, to struggle with it and then master it. They practice until their very cells absorb the music, and then twice a year, in May and December, the choral society welcomes the public to performances at the Belleville Church on High Street.

The group began singing during the grim depression years. They were years during which employees willingly took four or five wage cuts as long as they could bring home a paycheck, years when recent high school graduates stood almost no chance of finding a job, prompting a group of young women in Amesbury to put their energy and voices to a new venture, a choral society. Shortly thereafter, a group began singing in Newburyport, too, and they blended to form the Newburyport Choral Society, giving their first concert in 1935.

Singers come from many North Shore towns and all walks of life. They range in age from high school students to octogenarian Betty Gillette, who sang in the very first concert. The choral society inspires enormous loyalty both to the group as a whole and to one another. Members involve themselves in hours of volunteer work, from preparing mailings to organizing fund-raisers. One couple met through their musical connection and wed. More recently, when one woman heard that a friend from the choral society was undergoing dialysis and needed a kidney, she underwent tests and, upon learning she was a match, donated her kidney. The donor, a tenor, and the recipient, a soprano, are healthy and back singing with the group.

Two hundred members of the Newburyport Choral Society stand, and their voices begin to flow like streams cascading down a mountain until they join together in a glorious river of sound spilling over all those present and creating, in the words of a tenor, "a moment of grace."

A reunion of sorts

ℰↄ

The man and woman met across the buffet table at Harvard University, each there for a different event. "What did you say your name was?" she asked him as she filled her plate.

"Walter Atkinson," he replied. "And who are you?"

"I'm Elizabeth Martin."

He learned that she was from Newbury and expressed surprise. "The Atkinsons are from Newbury, too."

"When you've got your food," Elizabeth Martin told him, "I want to speak to you."

They sat to eat, and Ms. Martin introduced herself as the great-great-great-great-granddaughter of Goody Martin. Mr. Atkinson continued to look blank until he learned how their families were connected.

In the late 1600s Susannah Norse Martin lived in Amesbury across the Merrimack River. Recently widowed, she let it be known that some of her farm equipment and animals were up for sale. John Atkinson of Newbury took the ferry across and purchased one of her heifers. For some reason, he didn't bring it back with him that day, but he paid for it.

When he returned, the heifer was acting bizarrely, galloping wildly around the paddock and making it impossible for Atkinson to lasso her. He came back several times but could not claim his cow. Perhaps Goody Martin would not return his money. Some say she was annoyed because John had made the original transaction with her son, not her. She had quite a temper, which likely made a compromise problematic. The truth lies buried with them both. But Atkinson became so angry that he accused her of bewitching his heifer.

Some time later, Goody Martin came to the Atkinsons' home in the midst of a northeast storm. To plead with them? To reason? No one knows. Sara Atkinson was terrified when she saw "the witch" standing on her threshold. She allowed her to come in, but sent the children to other rooms for safety.

Subsequently the Atkinsons traveled to Salem, where all regional judicial proceedings took place, and condemned Goody Martin as a witch. They testified that though she had walked from Amesbury through pouring rain without bonnet or overshoes, she arrived at their home completely dry—obvious proof of her consorting with the devil.

Puritan authorities hanged Susannah Norse Martin for witchcraft on July 19, 1692. She was the only person north of the Merrimack who died during the witch hysteria.

Walter Atkinson sat shaken, his food untouched. While the Martin family had told and retold the story from one generation to the next, he could recollect hearing only vague references to what had occurred. What does an Atkinson say to a Martin three hundred years later? He found the right words, for ever since, Walter Atkinson and Elizabeth Martin, descendants of the accuser and the accused, have kept up a lively correspondence, though he lives on the opposite coast, in California.

Sources

"An account of the Great Fire" Newburyport: W. & J. Gilman, 1811.

"An account of the Historical Society's role in urban restoration." Historical Society of Old Newbury, 1978.

Atkinson, Minnie. *The First Religious Society of Newburyport.* News Publishing Co. Inc., 1933.

Bathe, Greville and Dorothy. *Jacob Perkins: His Invention, His Times, & His Contemporaries.* Philadelphia: Historical Society of Pennsylvania, 1943.

Benes, Peter. *Old-Town and the Waterside.* Historical Society of Old Newbury, 1986.

Blackington, Alton H. *Yankee Yarns.* New York: Dodd, Mead & Co., 1954.

Brown, Anne Augusta Fitch. "Diary for 1870." Edited and published by Agate Brown Collord, 1959.

Brown, Charles W. *My Ditty Bag.* Boston: Small, Maynard & Co., 1925.

Cheney, Robert K. *Maritime History of the Merrimack: Shipbuilding.* Newburyport: Newburyport Press, 1964.

Coffin, Elizabeth Hazen Little. "Reminiscences." 1901.

Coffin, Joshua. *A Sketch of the History of Newbury, Newburyport, and West Newbury.* Boston: S. G. Drake, 1845 Reprinted by Peter Randall, 1977.

———. Letter to his daughter Sarah, 18 August, 1839.

Comer, William R. *Landmarks in the Old Bay State.* 1911.

Currier, John J. *History of Newburyport 1764-1905.* Vols. 1–2. Newburyport, 1906. (Reprinted by New Hampshire Publishing Co., 1977)

———. *Ould Newbury: Historical and Biographical Sketches.* Boston: Damrell & Upham, 1896.

Cushing, T. C. "Account of the Short Life and Ignominious Death of Stephen Merrill Clark." Salem, 1821.

———. "Report of the Evidence, Arguments of Counsel, Charge and Sentence at the Trial of Stephen Merrill Clark for Arson before the Supreme Judicial Court." Salem, 1821.

Decatur, Stephen. "The Moulton Silversmiths." *Antiques.* January 1941.

Drake, Samuel Adams. *New England Legends.* Rutland, Vt.: Charles E. Tuttle Co., 1884. Reprinted by Little, Brown & Co. 1987.

Emery, Sarah Anna. *Reminiscences of a Newburyport Nonagenarian.* W. H. Huse, 1879. Reprinted by Heritage Books, 1978.

Fifer, J. Valerie. *William Wheelwright, Steamship and Railroad Pioneer.* Newburyport: Historical Society of Old Newbury, 1998.

Gillis, Andrew Joseph. "Me, 'Bossy' Gillis." *Boston Herald.* Jan. 16–29, 1928.

Grimke, Archibald H. *William Lloyd Garrison, the Abolitionist.* New York: Funk & Wagnalls, 1891. Reprinted AMS Press, 1974.

History of Essex County, Massaschusetts. Philadelphia: J. W. Lewis & Co., 1888.

History of the Marine Society. Compiled by Captain William Bayley and Captain Oliver O. Jones. Press of the Daily News, 1906.

Howe, Octavius T. & Frederick C. Matthews. *American Clipper Ships, 1833-1858.* New York: Argosy Antiquarian Ltd., 1967.

Howells, John Mead. *The Architectural Heritage of the Merrimack.* New York: Architectural Book Publishing Co., 1941. Reprinted by Heritage Books, 1978.

Jacobs, Peter H. *Front and Center: The Legend of Bossy Gillis.* Newburyport: Newburyport Press, Inc. 1968.

Krohn, J. A. *The Walk of Colonial Jack.* Newburyport, 1919.

Larson, David E., M.D., editor. *Mayo Clinic Family Health Book.* New York: William Morrow & Co., Inc., 1996.

Lord, John Lewis. Diary. Volumes 6–8. 1866.

Marquand, John P. *Timothy Dexter Revisited.* Boston: Little, Brown & Co., 1960.

———. *Wickford Point.* Boston: Little, Brown & Co., 1939.

Martingale, Hawser. *Tales of the Ocean.* New York: John Slater, 1840.

Merrill, Walter M. *Against Wind and Tide: A biography of William Lloyd Garrison.* Cambridge, MA.: Harvard University Press, 1963.

"Mysterious and terrible tragedy in the Merrimack House." Newburyport: J. P. Aubin, 1854.

Parsons, Fred W. "Once Upon a Time." Columns in the *Newburyport Daily News,* 1942.

Powers, Edwin. *Crime and Punishment in Early Massachusetts.* Boston: Beacon Press, 1966.

Ship's log from the *Whittier,* 1875.

Siebert, Wilbur H. *Underground Railroad in Massachusetts.* Worcester: American Antiquarian Society, 1936.

Smith, E. Vale. *History of Newburyport.* Newburyport, 1854. Reprinted by Parker River Researchers, Newburyport, 1983.

Tagney, Ronald N. *A County in Revolution.* Manchester, MA.: Cricket Press, 1976.

Willoughby, Malcolm F. *Rum War at Sea.* Washington: U.S. Government Printing Office, 1964.

Woodwell, Roland H. *John Greenleaf Whittier: A Biography.* Published under auspices of The Trustees of the John Greenleaf Whittier Homestead, Haverhill, , 1985.

———. "William Ashby of Newburyport and his Laurel Parties." Essex Institute Historical Collection, Volume 84. Jan.–Oct., 1948. Salem: Essex Institute, 1948.

Frequently consulted: *Newburyport Daily News, Newburyport Herald.*